ENCOUNTERING WORLD RELIGIONS
AN ORTHODOX CHRISTIAN PERSPECTIVE AND PARISH STUDY GUIDE

BY ALEXANDER GOUSSETIS

LIGHT & LIFE PUBLISHING MINNEAPOLIS, MN

Light & Life Publishing Company
P.O. Box 26421
Minneapolis, Minnesota 55426-0421

ISBN: 978-1-933654-22-5
Library of Congress Control Number: 2008932610

THIS BOOK IS DEDICATED TO

Lisa

"A good wife who can find? She is far more precious than jewels."
—Proverbs 31:10

AND

Julia, Nicholas, and Sophia

". . . your children will be like olive shoots around your table."
—Psalm 128:3

Table of Contents

Preface

In the spring of 2000, I was ready for a new challenge. As much as I enjoyed serving as pastor of the Archangel Michael Greek Orthodox Church in Campbell, Ohio, I missed the excitement of the university classroom. In the parish, one serves a homogenous group of people. For the most part, parishioners share similar religious beliefs, a common ethnicity, tried and true traditions, and a consistent worldview. But in the classroom one is immersed in a variety of ideologies, backgrounds, and personal expressions.

I followed up my passion for the classroom by applying for a part-time position at nearby Youngstown State University. The Chair of the Philosophy and Religious Studies department at YSU, Dr. Thomas Shipka, interviewed me and inquired as to my area of interest. I proposed an elementary class on Eastern Orthodoxy, knowing that there were at least four hundred students at YSU with an Orthodox Christian background.

Dr. Shipka was not encouraging regarding a class on Orthodoxy. Perhaps he saw me, as a pastor, geared more toward proselytizing students rather than offering an academic environment for learning. I countered by suggesting a course on Early Christian Writings or the New Testament. Still no success. Dr. Shipka kindly ended our conversation by saying that he would keep my resume/application on file.

Less than a month later, Dr. Shipka contacted me and extended an offer to teach a class on World Religions, which exactly fit my busy schedule. I readily agreed, thinking that at least I could get my foot in the door at YSU. If I proved myself worthy in the field of world religions, then I would be able to request again to instruct a class on Eastern Orthodoxy.

To my surprise, I thoroughly enjoyed teaching (and studying) world religions. It broadened my horizons and perspectives. In fact, the experience I had teaching at YSU made me a better pastor by allowing me to integrate the message of Orthodoxy into a worldly context for my parishioners.

Up to that point in my priesthood, I had encouraged my flock to read and learn about their Orthodox faith. As a result of teaching at YSU, I was adding a second challenge to my community; learn about world religions because we live in a pluralistic world. The axiom that I developed was this: "The more we learn about Orthodoxy, the more we can share our faith with the world around us. The more we Orthodox learn about other religions, the more effective we can be in dialoguing about the treasure of Orthodoxy."

As a result of my wonderful experience at YSU, I was encouraged to write a primer on world religions from an Orthodox perspective. Each chapter in this book focuses on one of the world religions, including an historical timeline, the basic teachings and key terms of that religion, and an Orthodox perspective of that faith. Also included in each chapter are selected writings from each religion, in order to give the reader a flavor of other sacred texts. Finally, reflection questions are offered at the conclusion of each chapter to encourage dialogue at parish study groups.

There are many people to thank for their contributions to this book.

- First I wish to express gratitude to Dr. Thomas Shipka, who was an excellent administrator and who always was complimentary to my teaching work at YSU.

- My heart and my love belong to the parish of Archangel Michael in Campbell, Ohio. The members of that pious community gave me their blessing to teach. In the seven years that I served that wonderful community, they helped me to grow as a pastor, a teacher, a Christian, a husband, and a father.

- To the community I now serve, Annunciation Orthodox Church in Lancaster, PA, I am grateful for the support and affection they have offered to my family. The parish in Lancaster embraces outreach, theological dialogue, and concern for others as a by product of their Orthodox faith.
- I am grateful to Dr. Anton Vrame and Rev. Demetrius Nicoloudakis for their stylistic recommendations and their friendships.
- Special thanks are extended to Rev. Anthony Coniaris, who is not only a prolific author but a gifted editor. He has the ability to guide potential writers in countless ways; he emboldens, he invigorates, he endorses discovery and endless possibilities. Rev. Coniaris was equally supportive in the publication of my first book, *Renewed Day by Day: An Orthodox Prayer Workbook* (Minneapolis, MN: Light & Life Publishing, 1997).

I must emphasize and underscore that this book is simply an introduction to other religions. There are numerous details and nuances in each faith that are not covered in this survey. Furthermore, the Orthodox perspective offered in this book is not meant to discredit or condemn any other faith; it is simply formatted to draw distinctions between Orthodox Christianity and other world religions.

Much of the information offered in this book about the various world religions was culled from the following sources:

Ludwig, Thomas M., *The Sacred Paths*, Third Edition. Upper Saddle River: Prentice Hall, 2001

Matthews, Warren, *World Religions*, Third Edition. Belmont, CA: Wadsworth Publishing, 1999.

Noss, David S., *A History of the World's Religions*, Eleventh Edition. Upper Saddle River: Prentice Hall, 2003

Smith, Huston N., *The Illustrated World's Religions*. San Francisco: Harper Collins, 1994.

I fully accept all responsibility for any errors in the text that do not fairly describe the religions covered. Much finer works than this volume will be written in the future by more accomplished authors in regard to how Orthodox Christianity relates to other religions. May this resource simply be a starting point in the education process as well as provide rudimentary material in conversations with people of other creeds.

—Rev. Dr. Alexander Goussetis, June 11, 2008

Introduction

What is religion? How does one approach the study of religion? Some consider religion to be *personal*; 'my relating to the holy' or 'my experience of the holy.' Others infer that religion has a *social* dimension; the effect that religion has on a society's culture, morals, government, etc. Still others view religion from the *conceptual* standpoint; objectively studying the history, doctrine, rituals, symbols, sacred writings, etc.

Since people understand and approach religion from so many vantage points, perhaps the place to begin our musings on the topic is to define the term *religion*, using three different sources. First, *Webster's New International Dictionary* defines religion as, "a personal awareness or conviction of the existence of a supreme being or of supernatural powers or influences controlling one's own, humanity's, or all of nature's destiny."

Second, Theodore Ludwig, author of the book, *Sacred Paths*, offers a four-part description of the word religion:

1) Religion is human involvement with what is considered to be the realm of the sacred.

2) It is expressed in thought, action, and social forms.

3) It constitutes a total system of symbols with deep meaning (words, ideas, rituals, pictures, gestures, and/or sounds).

4) It is a path of ultimate transformation.

A third definition of religion, and perhaps the most contemporary perspective, is offered by world religion author Dean Halverson, who counters:

Religion is a set of beliefs that answers the ultimate questions: What is ultimate reality? What is the nature of the world? What is the nature of humanity? What is humanity's primary problem? What happens after death?

Throughout the world, people are actively pursuing the study of 'ultimate questions.' Still others have little or no interest in religious thought. Regardless of which camp one may be in, the reality is that world events have been shaped by religion throughout history. Consider only a few examples of how religion has affected the world in the past two generations:

1940's Nazi Germany attempts to eliminate an entire group of religious peoples—the Jews

1960's Communist China suppresses all religion during the 'Cultural Revolution'

1970's Shah of Iran overthrown and Islamic group controls a nation (theocracy)

1990's Fall of communism; end of atheistic rule for many East European nations

2000's Events of September 11th, 2001 and the ramifications of the Iraq War

We live in a pluralistic and integrated world in which religion plays a vital role in interpreting world events. Thus, as Orthodox Christians, we must be informed about the history and theology of world religions. This book is not an exhaustive study of various world religions but simply a primer to encourage further research and dialogue.

Just as the fields of law and medicine have a vocabulary that is unique to their domain, religion also has a broad lexicon that one must become familiar with. The remainder of this introduction offers an elementary list of words that one must grasp before moving on to the study of world religions. Within each succeeding chapter, an additional group of terms will be defined, as it relates to that particular religion:

Asceticism – Self-discipline or self-denial for the purposes of growing in the spiritual life.

Agnosticism – Not the denial of the divine but "I don't know whether God exists or not," or, that if God exists, it is impossible for humans to know it.

Atheism – Non-belief in any deity.

Dogma – Systems of doctrines which define or describe a religious belief or community.

Ethics – Concerned with morality; right and wrong behavior; dogma that is applied in everyday life.

Fundamentalism – A literal reading and interpretation of scriptures, or dogma, or ritual, or ethics; letter of the law over spirit of the law.

Immanent – The belief that God is experiential and present in this world.

Monotheism – Belief in one almighty God, separate from the world.

Mystery – Something that has not been explained or cannot be explained; limitation of our human condition. No amount of scholarship can overcome it.

Philosophy – Humanistic, rational thinking. In contrast to theology, which is the study of the sacred.

Polytheism – Belief that many divine powers share in the world's operation.

Profane/Secular – Nonreligious or worldly.

Sacred – The realm of the extraordinary, the supernatural, the holy.

Syncretism – The belief that all religious paths possess equal truth.

Transcendent – The belief that God exists above and outside of the material universe.

PRIMAL RELIGIONS

PRIMAL RELIGIONS IN HISTORY

5000 BC	Agriculture and domesticated cattle in Nile Delta
4000	Intense hunting, gathering, fishing in Boreal regions
3000	Farming in Central Africa
2000	Metalworking in Peru
1500	Maize farming in Central America
300	Rise of Hopewell Chiefdoms in Illinois and Ohio
300 AD	Rise of Mayan Civilization
1200-1300	Eskimos appear in Greenland
1325-1470	Aztec and Inca Civilizations
1526-1870	Slaves shipped from Africa
1645	Tasman circumnavigates Australia
1880-1913	Western powers partition Africa

PRIMAL RELIGIONS

Holy Mother Earth, the trees and all nature are witnesses of your thoughts and deeds.
—A Winnebago Proverb

Throughout the world, pockets of people still follow local sacred ways handed down from their remote ancestors and adapted to contemporary circumstances. These groups of people, and their respective religions, are referred to as *indigenous*, *traditional*, *tribal*, or *primal* religions.

These primal religions comprise about four percent of the world population. This group maintains a sacred way of life that is distinctively different from all other religions. Mary Pat Fisher, in her book, *Living Religions*, notes that these primal religions "were almost lost under the onslaught of genocidal colonization, conversion pressures from global religions, mechanistic materialism, and destruction of their natural environments by the global economy of limitless consumption." Fortunately, there has been a renewal in recent times in better understanding these traditional expressions of faith.

In this chapter, we will consider an overview of indigenous peoples as a whole. However, behind these generalizations lie many differences in social contexts, as well as in religious beliefs and practices.

COMMON THEMES IN PRIMAL RELIGIONS

Immense variety and expression of faith

Indigenous religions are found in every corner of the world today. A brief survey of primal religions would include the Aborigine people of Australia, tribal groups in Africa, Eskimos (Inuits) in Greenland, Canada, and Alaska, and Indians in North and South America. Some are descendants of civilizations with advanced urban technologies that were needed to support concentrated populations. At the other end of the spectrum are those rural cultures that maintain a survival strategy of hunting and gathering.

Complexity and Sophistication of Religious Beliefs

Many people who have not grown up in native cultures attempt to embrace indigenous spiritual ways. However, 'outsiders' may not fully comprehend the context of primal religions, and often disrupt or alter indigenous practices. Osage theologian and author George Tinker, in his book *Missionary Conquest: The Gospel and Native American Genocide*, describes what often happens in North America:

The first Indian casualty today with outsiders is most often the strong deep cultural value of community and group cohesion that is important to virtually every indigenous people…Well meaning New Agers drive in from New York and Chicago or fly in from Austria and Denmark to participate in annual ceremonies originally intended to secure the wellbeing of the local Indian community. These visitors see little or nothing at all of the reservation community, pay little attention to the poverty and suffering of the people there, and finally leave having achieved only a personal, individual spiritual high.

Many native peoples are wary of this trend. They feel that their sacred ways are all they have left and worry that even these may be sold, stolen, and ruined.

Non-literate Oral Traditions
Most primal religions do not refer to sacred writings or have a comprehensive system of beliefs and doctrines. Their practices and traditions have been passed down orally from one generation to the next. The reality of a non-literate oral tradition has numerous ramifications, some that have strengthened and sustained primal religions, and some that have weakened and splintered these groups.

For example, one benefit of this non-literate and oral tradition is that it encourages communal interaction and interdependence. The face-to-face, person-to-person transmission of their respective faith in the form of stories, songs, rituals, dances, prayers, etc. brings about a circle of sacred relationships.

A second strength of non-literate oral traditions is the ability of indigenous peoples to retain an immense amount of information. Primal societies are not bookish or abstract or cut off from immediacy of the sacred. Their marvelous memories allow for an experiential component often missing from Western religions.

Unfortunately, there are hindrances to non-literate oral traditions. First and most obvious, there are limits to the potential size of a primal religion. If an indigenous group is a somewhat closed society, leery of outsiders, and little information is available about that group, the result is a dwindling or restricting number of adherents. Unlike Christianity or Islam, the mission component of primal religions is not evident.

A second, and debilitating, aspect of non-literate and oral traditions is that there are limits to economic and political influence that can be exercised. Historically, primal religions have not been able to advocate for themselves, whether it was the American Indians versus the United States government, or the tribes of Africa versus the colonial forces of Europe, among many examples.

Wholistic Reverence for Nature/Creation

Western or progressive peoples have tended to exploit nature for economic benefits. The reverent attitude of primal societies towards nature is bluntly expressed in this passage from T. C. McLuhan, in the book *Touch the Earth*:

The White people never cared for land or deer or bear. When we Indians kill meat, we eat it all up. When we dig roots we make little holes. When we build houses, we make little holes. When we burn grass for grasshoppers, we don't ruin things. We shake down acorns and pine nuts. We don't chop down trees. We only use dead wood. But the White people plow up the ground, pull down the trees, kill everything. The tree says, "Don't. I am sore. Don't hurt me." But they chop it down and cut it up. The spirit of the land hates them. They blast out trees and stir it up to its depths. They saw up the trees.

That hurts them. The Indians never hurt anything, but the White people destroy all…How can the spirit of the earth like the White man?…Everywhere the White man has touched, it is sore.

AN ORTHODOX PERSPECTIVE OF PRIMAL RELIGIONS

One finds many areas of common ground between Orthodox Christianity and primal religions: the understanding of a Creator God; the interdependence between God, humanity and creation; the emphasis on community; the acceptance of mystery in life and faith; the use of rituals and symbols in worship; the remembrance and reverence for ancestors, among others. The emphasis on the remaining section of the Orthodox perspective will focus on the role of nature and creation.

The Orthodox view of creation is not based on anthropocentrism but theocentrism – the view that, at the center of all is God. The world was created by the will of God. Creation is therefore a free act; a gratuitous act of God. St. Gregory of Nyssa writes:

All creation, both the comprehensible and concerning the sensible nature, is created from non-being; all that exists is by God's will. God created this world, that is to say, that in which all creation is conceived, visible and invisible.

While Orthodox dogma states that humankind was made in the image of God, the same is not true about nature and God. However, humans relate directly to creation as well as to the Creator. There is implied a balance within nature, inasmuch as nature includes humankind. This image is expressed vividly by the Alexandrian theologian, Origen, who wrote:

As a body is an organism made up of many members, and it is held together by one soul, so, in my opinion, the whole world is a kind of huge immense living creature which, is united by one soul, namely the power and reason of God.

This harmonious perspective between humankind, creation, and God is found extensively in Scripture. In the Psalms alone are at least three references:

1) Nature reflects the almighty majesty and goodness of God: "The earth is the Lord's, and the fullness thereof; the world and they that dwell therein" (Ps. 24:1).

2) The creation of the world is not an act of divine will which took place in the distant past, but a constantly continuing process: "You send forth your spirit and they are created; and You renew the face of the earth" (Ps. 104:30).

3) Concerning the responsibility of humankind for the future of the earth: "Mercy and truth are met together; righteousness and peace have kissed each other. Truth shall spring out of the earth; and righteousness shall look down from heaven. Yes, the Lord shall give that which is good; and our land shall yield her increase" (Ps. 85:10-12).

Related to #3 above is this important passage from Genesis, in which God makes clear to Adam and Eve: "You may freely eat of every tree of the garden; but of the tree of the knowledge of good and evil you shall not eat" (Genesis 2:16-17). This is a profound sentence with many meanings, but among them is the idea that there are limits to our use of creation; limits set upon us by God. This command, in symphony with primal religions, requires that we replace mindless consumerism with a way of life which is outwardly simple but inwardly rich.

The attitude of the Orthodox faith to nature is not to compartmentalize or to isolate matter and spirit. Rather, the Church views reality wholistically. As a result, spiritual activity is not antithetical to material. This is exhibited in the many things used in Orthodox corporate prayers – icons, candles, oil lamps, incense, bread, wine, oil, water, etc.

One practical illustration of this is during the celebration of the Baptism of Jesus Christ, or Epiphany. The ecological dimension of the faith becomes clearer when the element of water, so essential for all of nature, is perceived as an avenue towards the goal of deification. Creation is viewed as participating in Christ's saving work. Water becomes a vehicle for saving and sanctification. One of the hymns of the feast expresses this symbolic view of the sanctified water: "…let us run to the undefiled fountains of the stream of salvation."

While there is a distinction made between the spiritual and material world, there is no sharp separation or contradiction between them either. The spiritual and the material form one reality, God's creation. This unity is expressed clearly in another hymn of the feast of Epiphany: "Grant to all those who touch it, who anoint themselves with it or drink from it, sanctification, blessing, cleansing, and health."

KEY TERMS

Animist – One who believes that the trees, rocks, rivers, plants, and animals are spiritually alive; belief that the spirits that exist in nature have the power to help or harm. Therefore animists offer some form of worship to these spirits. This term is often applied to Native American religions.

Henotheism – A belief that one deity is supreme over other deities.

Myth – A storied explanation that portrays deities acting beyond the constraints of space and time (e.g. creation myths). In religious studies, myth does not mean that something is untrue.

Rites of Passage – ceremonies (rituals) of the life cycle; religious dramas for birth, puberty, marriage, death, etc. A new stage of development is marked with a new stage of intimacy with the sacred.

Ritual – Ceremonial action designed to express a people's beliefs, fears, and hopes. Indigenous rituals allow people to participate in their myths, making a psychosomatic impact.

Shaman – Those who offer themselves as mystical intermediaries between the physical and nonphysical world. They lead rituals that enable them to control spirits, often for purposes of healing.

Totem – An animal, plant, or other object serving as the symbol of a traditional people's clan or tribe. Totems are seen as 'helpers'. For example, an eagle could be a messenger from heaven, as well as a symbol of freedom or speed.

SELECTED WRITINGS

Pygmy, Africa

In the beginning was God,
   Today is God
   Tomorrow will be God.
Who can make an image of God?
He has no body.
He is as a word
   which comes out of your mouth.

Ute, North America

Earth teach me stillness
   as the grasses are stilled with light.
Earth teach me suffering
   as old stones suffer with memory.
Earth teach me humility
   as blossoms are humble with beginning.
Earth teach me caring
   as the mother who secures her young.
Earth teach me courage
   as the tree which stands all alone.
Earth teach me limitation
   as the ant which crawls on the ground.
Earth teach me freedom
   as the eagle which soars in the sky.
Earth teach me resignation
   as the leaves which die in the fall.
Earth teach me regeneration
   as the seed which rises in the spring.
Earth teach me to forget myself
   as the melted snow forgets its life.
Earth teach me to remember kindness
   as dry fields weep with rain.

Ngombe, Central Africa

Akongo was not always as he is now. In the beginning the creator lived among men; but men were quarrelsome. One day they had a big quarrel and Akongo left them to themselves. He went and hid in the forest and nobody has seen him since. People today can't tell what he is like.

Teton Sioux, North America

Perhaps you have noticed that even in the very lightest breeze you can hear the voice of the cottonwood tree; this we understand is its prayer to the Great Spirit, for not only men, but all things and all beings pray to Him continually in differing ways.

For the Great Spirit is everywhere; he hears whatever is in our minds and hearts, and it is not necessary to speak to Him in a loud voice.

Since the drum is often the only instrument used in our sacred rites, I should perhaps tell you here why it is especially sacred and important to us. It is because the round form of the drum represents the whole universe, and its steady strong beat is the pulse, the heart, throbbing at the center of the universe. It is as the voice of *Wakan-Tanka*, and this sound stirs us and helps us to understand the mystery and power of all things.

QUESTIONS FOR REFLECTION

1) What are the most important human concerns addressed by primal religions? How does the Orthodox faith address human concerns?

2) How does profanity, the lack of sacredness, influence contemporary Western culture? Is Orthodoxy compatible with Western culture, with any culture?

3) Who understands a religion better, an insider (someone practicing the faith) or an outsider (someone outside the faith)? Which is in a better position to compare the religion with others?

4) What lasting impressions do you have of primal religions? What questions remain for further study?

HINDUISM

HINDUISM IN HISTORY

1500 BC	Aryan migration into northern India
1200	Beginning of creation of the Vedas
800	Beginning of creation of the Upanishads
200BC-200AD	Laws of Manu and Bhagavad Gita written
788-820	Life of philosopher Shankara
1200	Muslim entry into northern India
1757	British rule established in Calcutta
1858	British control government of India
1920	Mohandas K. Gandhi leads Indian National Congress
1947	India achieves independence from Britain

HINDUISM

I am proud to belong to a religion which has taught the world both tolerance and universal acceptance. We believe not only in universal tolerance, but we accept all religions as true. As different streams having different sources all mingle their waters in the sea, so different paths which men take through different tendencies various though they appear, crooked or straight, all lead to God.

—Swami Vivekananda

Perhaps the oldest and most complex of all the religions of the world is Hinduism. It is probably the most diverse and varied of all religions. Diana Eck, a religion scholar, writes that Hinduism "is a non-centralized, evolving composite of variegated ways of worship, with as many ways to the ultimate as there are people."

Mary Pat Fisher, author of *Living Religions*, writes the following about Hinduism:

> The spiritual expressions of Sanatana Dharma (Hinduism) range from extreme asceticism to extreme sensuality, from the heights of personal devotion to a deity to the heights of abstract philosophy, from metaphysical proclamations of the oneness behind the material world to worship of images representing a multiplicity of deities. According to tradition, there are actually three hundred thirty-three million deities in India. The feeling is that the Divine has countless faces, and all are divine.

Unlike most of the other major religions of the world, Hinduism has no identifiable founder. Although there have been many influential teachers and leaders in its history, there has never been one whose teachings became the wellspring of all later Hindu thought.

Because of the tremendous complexities in grasping basic Hindu thought, we will limit our focus to three specific areas: sacred writings, key terms that express important theological characteristics, and the four main types of *yoga* which leads one to the ultimate.

EARLY HISTORY AND EARLY SACRED WRITINGS

Around 2000-1500BC it is believed that a group of people migrated into India from the northwest. They brought with them their own religion, which would make its distinctive contribution to what would later be known as Hinduism. These people called themselves Aryans, their word for 'noble.' Aryan religion consisted of worship of polytheistic gods who were believed to control the forces of nature. Worship of the gods took place at outdoor fire altars. Sacred chants, which the priests knew from memory, were an essential part of the ceremonies. It is these chants, eventually placed in written form, that make up the core of the Aryan's earliest sacred literature, called the *Vedas*. Although many of the Aryan gods are no longer worshipped, elements of the Aryan religion continue to be of great importance to Hindus today.

The *Vedas* are the earliest sacred books of Hinduism. The name means 'knowledge' or 'wisdom.' Although scholars date the earliest versions of the *Vedas* to be about 1500-1200BC, pious Hindus consider them to be far more ancient.

There are four basic sacred text collections that constitute the *Vedas*. The *Rig Veda* ('hymn knowledge') is a collection of more than a thousand chants to the Aryan gods; the *Yajur Veda* ('ceremonial knowledge') contains matter for recitation during sacrifice; the *Sama Veda* ('chant knowledge') is a handbook of musical elaborations of Vedic chants; and the *Atharva Veda* ('knowledge from the teacher') consists of practical prayers and charms, such as prayers to protect against snakes and sickness.

The *Rig Veda*, the most important of the *Vedas*, has an account of the origin of the universe. The universe is said to have emerged from a division and cosmic sacrifice of a primeval superperson, *Purusha*. But the account includes a touching admission of uncertainty:

> Who knows it for certain; who can proclaim it here; namely, out of what it was born and wherefrom his creations issued? The gods appeared only later – after the creation of the world. Who knows, then, out of what it has evolved?

The *Vedas* usually include these four collections. However, detailed ceremonial rules, called *Brahmanas* and *Aranyakas*, were added by later generations to each of the four Vedic collections. Still later works were added to the Vedas, called the *Upanishads*, which express philosophical and religious ideas that arose in introspective and meditative traditions.

Two other collections of Hindu sacred writings, written much later than the *Vedas*, need also be highlighted. First is the *Ramayana*, written between 400-200BC. The *Ramayana* is a long poetic narrative in the Sanskrit language. It is a much beloved text that is acted out with great pageantry throughout India every year. It depicts the duties of relationships (servant, brother, wife, etc.).

The other sacred writing is entitled *Mahabharata*, which is an epic poem of over 100,000 verses composed between 400BC-400AD. This influential scripture includes the *Bhagavad Gita*, a treatise on the nature of faith, which brings conflict between our earthly duties and our spiritual aspirations.

KEY TERMS/THEOLOGICAL CHARACTERISTICS

Reincarnation

Beginning in the Upanishads, death is not seen as an endpoint to life. Individuals are understood as manifestations of the Divine Spirit, which does not end when the individual dies. They are the continuation of earlier forms of life that have simply taken new forms. Hinduism generally adopts the belief that everything living has its own life force and that every life force, when it loses one form, is reborn into another. This process is known as reincarnation.

Karma

Hinduism's concept of rebirth assumes that human beings have at one or another time existed as a 'lower' form, such as animal, insect, and possibly even plant. Human beings are also capable of achieving 'higher' forms of life, such as superhuman beings and demigods. Rebirth can move in either direction, and the human stage is a dangerous one because each person must make dramatic choices about how to live. What determines the direction of one's rebirth is *karma*. The word comes from a root that means 'to do' and implies the notion of moral consequences that are carried along with every act. *Karma* is the moral law and effect. Belief in karma is a belief that every action has an automatic moral consequence.

Samsara

The term *samsara* refers to the wheel of life, the cycle of constant rebirth. Hindus believe an individual is constantly being reborn, having come from different earlier forms and going on to emerge in new forms in the future. *Samsara* continues until one achieves liberation, or *moksha*, which is union with *Brahman*, the ultimate reality. In the next section, we will elaborate on *yogas*, or means of achieving *moksha*.

Moksha

The term *moksha* means 'freedom' or 'liberation' and comes from a root that means 'to be released.' In the *Upanishads*, *moksha* is the ultimate human goal. *Moksha* includes the notion of getting beyond egotistical responses, such as resentment and anger, which limit the individual. As one becomes freer, one looks at life less from a selfish point of view and more from a perspective that embraces the whole. The unity and sacredness that everything shares becomes a part of everyday experience. Kindness to all creation is one natural result of this new insight, and kind actions also generate helpful *karma*. Detaching oneself from pleasure or pain is another practice that leads to freedom from egotism. When insight and kindness are ideal, at last the pain of rebirth ends; the limitations of individuality are gone, and only *Brahman* remains. The *Upanishads* explains complete freedom: "when all has become Spirit, one's own Self, how and whom could one see?"

FOUR MAIN TYPES OF *YOGAS*

Although the *Bhagavad Gita* endorses quiet contemplation, it also recommends active spiritual paths. The various types of *yogas* are methods that can be used to help people live spiritually. The word *yoga* means 'uniting together' or 'placing under discipline.' A *yoga* is a way for people to perfect their union with the divine, and because the *yogas* suggest roads to perfection, they are also called *margas* (paths). There is a recognition in Hinduism that different sorts of people need different spiritual paths, and an individual's personality type will help determine the appropriate *yoga* to practice. The four main expressions of *yoga* are as follows:

Jnana Yoga ('knowledge yoga')
This type of *yoga* brings insight into one's divine nature by studying the *Upanishads* and the *Bhagavad Gita* and their commentaries and by learning from *gurus* who have attained insight. *Jnana yoga* is particularly appropriate for priests and intellectuals.

Karma Yoga ('action yoga')
This type of *yoga* proposes that all useful work, if done unselfishly, can be a way to perfection. (The word *karma* here is used in its basic sense of 'activity.') Much of what we ordinarily do is motivated by money or pleasure or praise, but deeds performed without a desire for reward are the heart of *karma yoga*. The *Bhagavad Gita* states: "Desire for the fruits of work must never be your motive in working."

Bhakti Yoga ('devotion yoga')
Hinduism, because of its belief in multiple gods, offers rich possibilities for devotion. In the *Bhagavad Gita*, one reads, "Regard me as your dearest loved one. Know me to be your only refuge." *Bhakti yoga* can involve various

expressions of devotion – most commonly chants, songs, food offerings, and the anointing of statues.

Raja Yoga ('royal yoga')

This type of *yoga* promotes meditation and psychophysical exercises. It combines physical posturing, breathing positions, clearing the mind of distractions, and/ or the use of a word or brief phrase, called a *mantra*. In the *Upanishads*, one reads, "When all the senses are stilled, when the mind is at rest, when the intellect wavers not – that, say the wise, is the highest state."

In addition to these four *yogas* are others. In fact, any set of techniques that leads to greater spirituality can be considered a *yoga*.

THE CASTE SYSTEM

We cannot conclude this survey of Hinduism without briefly mentioning the controversial caste system. The caste system, the prevalent social system of the Aryans, had already been mentioned in the *Rig Veda*. It receives further religious approval in the *Bhagavad Gita*, which recognizes that there are different types of people and that their ways to perfection will differ, depending on their personality type and role in society.

Traditionally, the caste system was based on more than one's type of work, and in modern times it does not always indicate the type of work a person does. Castes are really social classes which dissuade members of different castes from interacting. Members of society are divided into five main social classes:

1) Intellectual and Spiritual leaders
2) Administrators, Organizers, and the Royal Aristocracy
3) Merchants, Landowners, Moneylenders, and sometimes Artisans

4) Unskilled Laborers
5) The 'Untouchables' who traditionally do the dirtiest work – cleaning toilets, sweeping streets, tanning animal hides.

What was probably an early concern for hygiene led to the separation of untouchables from the rest of society. They have often been forced to live in ghettos and sometimes have been horribly mistreated. Their low status prompted the Indian reformer Mohandas Gandhi to promote another name for their class, 'Children of God.' He urged their inclusion in regular society.

AN ORTHODOX PERSPECTIVE ON HINDUISM

Distinction between Creator and Creation

According to Hindu theology, the goal of life is to unite one's individual self, or *atman*, to the ultimate reality, or *Brahman*. This concept implies that there is no distinction between the creator and creation. Both are seen as one and the same. In Hinduism, when one achieves *moksha*, or liberation, at the time of their death that person then merges into Oneness; one's unique personhood disappears.

The Orthodox Christian response to this theology begins with the opening statement of the Nicene Creed: "I believe in one God, the Father Almighty, Creator of heaven and earth, and all things visible and invisible." Orthodox theology clearly submits that the world was created by the will of God. It is of another nature than God. It exists outside of God. Creation *ex nihilo* (out of nothing) is a dogma of the Christian faith: "Behold the heavens and the earth, and seeing all that is there, you will understand that God has created it from nothing" (Maccabees 7:28). Creation is therefore a free act, a gratuitous act of God.

St. John of Damascus, in his *Exact Exposition of the Orthodox Faith* offers this brilliant articulation:

Therefore, we believe in one God: one principle, without beginning, uncreated, indestructible and immortal, eternal, unlimited, unbounded, infinite in power, unchanging, constant, source of goodness and justice, power which is not subject to any measure, but which is measured only by His own will, for He can do all things whatsoever He pleases …one essence, one Godhead, one power, one will, one operation, one authority, one dominion, one kingdom, known in three perfect Hypostases (Persons), and known and worshipped with one worship.

The distinction between God and His creation is absolute. Humankind is made in the image of God, yet is distinguished from its Creator. God has specific attributes that separate Him from all of creation:

God is Eternal – The existence of God is outside of time. For God there is neither past nor future; there is only the present: "In the beginning, O Lord, You did lay the foundations of the earth, and the heavens are the works of Your hands" (Psalm 101:26).

God is All-Good – The goodness of God extends to all of creation and all the beings that exist in it: "Compassionate and merciful is the Lord, longsuffering and plenteous in mercy" (Psalm 102:8).

God is Omniscient – The knowledge of God is unlimited, yet does not violate the free will of creatures: "All things are naked and opened unto the eyes of Him" (Hebrews 4:13).

God is Almighty – God is the creator of the world, the all-governing: "He spoke, and they came into being; He commanded and they were created" (Psalm 32:9).

Reincarnation vs. Resurrection

One of the cornerstones of Eastern religions in general, and Hinduism in particular, is the concept of reincarnation. Restated briefly, reincarnation into a living being on earth occurs repeatedly until one is liberated or released from the cycle of life and united with *Brahman*, the ultimate reality.

Reincarnation is not compatible with Orthodox Christian theology. Instead, each human person is seen as a unique and unrepeatable creation by God. While death is also seen as a release from life on earth, Christians place their hope in the resurrection of Jesus Christ, and entrance into the kingdom of heaven. St. Gregory the Theologian writes:

> Every good and God-beloved soul, when it has been released by death from the body with which it was united, immediately experiences the joy and pleasures which it shall enjoy in full measure in the future …and though immediately after death the enjoyment is small, after, when it shall again receive its body at the resurrection of the dead, it shall enjoy blessings in perfect measure.

The following prayer, written by St. Ambrose of Milan, also makes vivid the uniqueness of every human being and the continuation of love relationships that began in one's earthly life and carries through in the kingdom of heaven:

> Lord God, we can hope for others nothing better than the happiness we desire for ourselves. Therefore, I pray to You, do not separate me after death from those I tenderly loved on earth. Grant that where I am, they may be with me, and that I may enjoy their presence in heaven…After this brief life on earth, give them eternal happiness.

The resurrection of the dead through Jesus Christ is the definitive theological component of Christianity. A basic understanding of this fundamental doctrine is essential for all Christians. In Kyriacos Markides' sequel to *The Silent Mountain*, entitled *Gifts of the Desert*, Father Maximos elaborates on the Orthodox exegesis of the resurrection and its impact on humankind:

> A human being is a psychosomatic unity, made of body and soul. The death of the body is an abnormal phenomenon, an affront to and degeneration of God's perfect work. For this reason God does not allow death to become victorious at the end. Through an eventual resurrection, God restores the unity of body and soul that was put asunder as a result of death…The soul never dies. It is only the dead body that will be resurrected in a new, imperishable and incorruptible form, just like Christ's body after the resurrection. Human beings will then be in a position to experience the joy of the Uncreated Glory of God not only as souls but also as a psychosomatic unity.

KEY TERMS

Atman – The individual self, held by Upanishadic and Vedantic thought to be identical with Brahman, the world-soul.

Bhakti – An Indian term for devotional worship to a deity centered on love.

Brahman – Hindu term for ultimate reality. Also understood as a creator god.

Dharma – One's religious and social duty, including both righteousness and faith.

Guru – One's teacher in Hindu spiritual practices.

Jnana – oneness with god through knowledge and reflection.

Karma – One's actions, whose cumulative result is held to have a determining effect on the quality of rebirth in future existences.

Mahabharata – A very long epic poem, containing the Bhagavad Gita as a portion of the text.

Mantra – An expression of one or more syllables, chanted repeatedly as a focus of concentration in meditation.

Moksha – The Hindu term for release and liberation from the cycle of life (*samsara*).

Reincarnation – The concept that a person's being survives after death and returns to animate a new body, usually in a nearly endless, cyclical way.

Samsara – The continuing cycle of rebirths.

Sanatana Dharma – The Indian term for Hinduism. It is loosely translated as 'eternal religion,' but also implies matters of duty, social welfare, and health.

Upanishads – Philosophical texts, in the form of reported conversations reflecting on the nature of knowledge.

Vedas – The four collections of hymns and ritual texts, constituting the oldest and most highly respected Hindu sacred literature.

Yoga – A pattern of practice and discipline, which can involve a philosophical system and mental concentration as well as physical postures and exercises.

SELECTED WRITINGS

Early Vedas

To gain thy mercy, Varuna, with hymns we bind thy
    heart, as binds the charioteer his tethered horse.
Varuna knows the path of birds that fly through
    heaven, and, sovereign of the sea, he knows the
    ships that are thereon.
He knows the pathway of the wind, the spreading, high
    and mighty wind; he knows the gods who dwell
    above.
Varuna, true to holy law, sits down among his people;
    he, most wise, sits there to govern all.
He beholds all wonderful things, both what has been,
    and hereafter will be done.

(Varuna is the Hindu omniscient God and protector of the moral order
of the world)

From the Upanishads

Awake, arise! Strive for the Highest, and be in the Light!
Sages say the path is narrow and difficult to tread, narrow as
the edge of a razor.

The Atman is beyond sound and form, without touch
and taste and perfume. It is eternal, unchangeable,
without beginning or end: indeed above reasoning. When
consciousness of the Atman manifests itself, man becomes
free from the jaws of death.

When the five senses and the mind are still, and reason
rests in silence, then begins the Path supreme. This calm
steadiness of the senses is called Yoga. Then one should
become watchful, because Yoga comes and goes. When
all desires that cling to the heart are surrendered, then a
mortal becomes immortal, and even in this world he is one

with Brahman. When all the ties that bind the heart are unloosened, then a mortal becomes immortal. This is the sacred teaching.

As rivers flowing into the ocean find their final peace and their name and form disappear, even so the wise become free from name and form and enter into the radiance of the Supreme Spirit who is greater than all greatness. In truth, who knows Brahman becomes Brahman.

(on reincarnation)

The soul is born and unfolds in a body, with dreams and desires and the food of life. And then it is reborn in new bodies, in accordance with its former works. The quality of the soul determines its future body: earthly or airy, heavy or light. Its thoughts and its actions can lead it to freedom, or lead it to bondage, in life after life. But there is the God of forms Infinite, and when a man knows God he is free from all bondage.

From the Bhagavad Gita

Death is certain for the born. Rebirth is certain for the dead. You should not grieve for what is unavoidable. Before birth, beings are not manifest to our human senses. In the interim between birth and death, they are manifest. At death they return to the unmanifest again. What is there in all this to grieve over?

(on the indestructibility of the soul/reincarnation/samsara)

It is not born, it does not die; having been, it will never not be; unborn, enduring, constant, and primordial, it is not killed when the body is killed. When a man knows the self to be indestructible, enduring, unborn, unchanging, how does he kill or cause anyone to kill?

QUESTIONS FOR REFLECTION

1) What evidence could you offer to support a belief in reincarnation? What evidence could you offer to weaken a belief in reincarnation?

2) What doctrines or practices of Hindus do you think are most misunderstood by non-Hindus?

3) Would Hinduism be seen as a more tolerant religion than Orthodox Christianity? Why or why not? Stated another way, can Orthodox Christianity be viewed as an exclusive religion?

4) Do the four main paths of Hindu transformation, or *yogas*, have any Orthodox Christian parallels?

5) What comparisons can you offer between the Hindu understanding of *karma* and the Christian understanding of sin?

BUDDHISM

BUDDHISM IN HISTORY

563-483 BC   Life of Siddhartha Gautama, the Buddha

273-232   Life of Ashoka, Indian king who spread Buddhism

200   Mahayana Buddhism begins rise

50 AD   Entry of Buddhism into China

400   Entry of Buddhism into Korea

552   Buddhism enters Japan under reign of Emperor Kimmei

630   Entry of Buddhism into Tibet

845   Third great persecution of Buddhism in China, which permanently weakened Chinese Buddhism

1000   Revival of Theravada Buddhism in Sri Lanka and Southeast Asia

1200   Beginning of the growth of Zen in Japan

1617   Dalai Lamas become rulers in Tibet

1900   Beginning of Buddhist missionary activity in the West

1959   Chinese takeover of Tibet, destroying temples and monasteries; Dalai Lama and other Tibetans flee to India

BUDDHISM

Let therefore, no man love anything;
loss of the beloved is evil. Those who love nothing
and hate nothing, have no fetters.
                    —Words Attributed to the Buddha

India in the sixth century before Christ was a state of religious fervor. There was great enthusiasm for religious experience, leading people to experiment with a variety of Hindu practices and to study with gurus. Into this cauldron of spiritual liberation came Siddhartha Gautama, who would come to be known as the Buddha, or the 'Awakened One.'

Because so many legends have surrounded the biography of Gautama, it is sometimes difficult to separate fact from fiction. What is generally accepted is that he was born in present day Nepal to wealthy parents. Gautama's mother died soon after his birth. His father sought to protect him from the ugliness and distress of humanity, thus keeping the boy safely behind a large walled palace compound. As a result, Gautama grew up surrounded by youth, beauty, and health. He married a young woman his father had chosen, and had a son.

All was proceeding according to his father's plan until Gautama disobeyed his father's command not to leave the palace grounds. Visiting the neighboring areas, he soon witnessed the suffering of ordinary life. He saw – and was moved by – what are called the Four Moving Sights. He came across a bent elderly man, a man with a loathsome disease, a rotting corpse, and finally, a monk who had no possessions but seemed to be at peace.

Gautama decided to leave the life he knew behind. Legend tells how he quietly said farewell to his sleeping wife and child. Then he took his best horse and rode off into the night. He clipped off his long hair and beard and sent his horse back. Putting on simple clothing, he began a period of searching for answers to life's miseries.

At first, Gautama thought the answers to the questions that troubled him were to be found in the various schools of religion and philosophy. Therefore, he attached himself to a guru and studied with him for some time. Gautama attempted techniques of meditation and strict asceticism, but to no avail. He remained unsatisfied in his search for truth, particularly in regard to suffering and death.

Disappointed by his spiritual attempts to this point, Gautama went to the banks of a river and sat down under the shade of a fig tree and began to meditate. During this time, he was said to have received enlightenment. In his meditation, Gautama had a vision of the endless cycle of birth and death that is the fate of humankind. He came to understand that people were bound to this cycle because of *tanha* (desire, thirst, craving). It is desire that causes *karma* and thus causes suffering. The Buddha had desired enlightenment and had sought it through asceticism and knowledge, but it eluded him. When he had ceased to desire it, he found enlightenment.

After this experience of enlightenment, the Buddha traveled in search of his former ascetical companions whom he spurned. He found them at Deer Park near Benares, and shared with them his newfound wisdom. The ascetics, noting the change that had come over the Buddha, reconciled and became the first *sangha* (community of disciples).

The Buddha spent the rest of his life traveling from village to village in northeast India, teaching his insights and his way of life. He attracted many followers, men and women, and from every caste found in India. The Buddha reportedly died at the age of eighty. According to tradition, his final words were, "subject to decay are all component things. Strive earnestly to work out your own salvation."

THE BASIC TEACHINGS OF BUDDHISM

It is impossible to know exactly what the Buddha taught. He did not write down his teachings, nor did his early disciples. The only written versions were recorded several hundred years after his death, following centuries of being passed on orally.

At the core of what is generally regarded as basic Buddhism are the Three Jewels; the Buddha, the *Dharma*, and the *Sangha*. The Buddha is thought of as an ideal human being whom other human beings should imitate, especially in the areas of self-control and mindfulness. The *Dharma* means the sum total of Buddhist teachings about how to view the world and how to live properly. These teachings can be summed up in the Four Noble Truths and the Noble Eightfold Path. The *Sangha*, as highlighted earlier, is the community of disciples.

THE FOUR NOBLE TRUTHS

Tradition states that in Deer Park, the Buddha delivered his first message. Essentially he presented the middle path between two extremes of self-indulgence and self-mortification. He went on to list the four truths of his enlightenment:

1) **To Live is to Suffer**.
   To live means to experience anxiety, loss, and sorrow. We may be happy for a while but happiness is not permanent. What one regards as *self* or *soul* is simply an ever-changing bundle of fleeting feelings, sense impressions, and ideas. Although this point may sound dark, the Buddha simply attempted to recognize why suffering comes about and then try to lessen it.

2) **Suffering (Dukkha) Originates in our Desires**.
   The term *tanha* translates into 'grasping,' 'craving,' or 'coveting.' Simple desires do not cause suffering but deep craving to make permanent what is impermanent is the cause of suffering. Everything is actually impermanent; changing all the time. The human person seeks to grasp and hold life as we want it to be, but cannot, since everything is in constant flux.

3) Stopping Desire Will Stop Suffering.
When one lessens desires and accepts freely the flow of life, suffering is reduced. The only way to end the cycle in which desire feeds the wheel of suffering is to end all cravings and lead a passion-free life. Doing so leads one into a state of *nirvana* (end of suffering; inner peace). Another way of stating this maxim is this: I cannot change the outside world, but I can change myself and the way I experience the world.

4) Release from Suffering is Possible and Can Be Attained by Following the Noble Eightfold Path.
The Buddha taught that only through a life of wisdom, moral conduct, and contemplation, highlighted in the Noble Eightfold Path, can desire and therefore suffering be extinguished.

THE EIGHTFOLD PATH OF LIBERATION

1) **Right understanding** – would include knowing the Four Noble Truths of existence and the doctrine of impermanence. If we think and act from a purified, trained mind, happiness will always follow us.

2) **Right thoughts or intentions** – is the freeing ourselves from the conditions of craving by cultivating the virtues of selflessness, goodwill, and compassion for all beings

3) **Right speech** – this precept cautions against vain talk, gossip, harsh words, and lying, and instead aims for speaking kindly and in friendly ways.

4) **Right action** – observes the five basic conditions for moral conduct: avoid destroying life, stealing, sexual misconduct, lying, and intoxicants.

5) **Right livelihood** – being sure that one's way of making a living does not violate the five conditions highlighted above. One's trade should not harm others or disrupt social harmony.

6) **Right effort** – means achieving a strong will that prevents and gets rid of wrong states of mind and creates and develops wholesome states of mind.

7) **Right mindfulness** – is particularly characteristic of Buddhism, for the way to liberation is said to be through the mind; actively mindful of all sensation, feelings, and thoughts.

8) **Right meditation/concentration** – is the attainment, through meditation, of higher stages of mental awareness by direct insight and enlightenment. The various schools of Buddhism that have developed over the centuries have taught different techniques of meditation, but this basic principle remains the same.

Although they are often called 'steps,' the eight recommendations are not to be practiced sequentially but rather all together. Notice the groupings of the eight steps; the first three refer to wisdom, the next three involve moral conduct, and the final three highlight contemplation.

BUDDHISM AFTER THE BUDDHA

In the first centuries after the Buddha's death, many Buddhist schools and splinter groups arose. Most of these ultimately died out and are only names to us today. A few survived and crystallized into the major branches of Buddhism that we recognize: *Theravada*, *Mahayana*, and *Tibetan* (sometimes called *Tantric* Buddhism).

Theravada Buddhism 'Way of the Elders'

Theravada Buddhism is the more conservative of the three groups (perhaps 38% of all Buddhists). As such, it believes itself to be closer to the original teachings of the Buddha. According to this branch of Buddhism, people must achieve enlightenment for themselves without reliance on the gods or on any other force beyond themselves. Thus the ideal practitioner of Theravadan Buddhism is a monk who shaves his head, puts on a yellow robe, takes up a begging bowl, and seeks release from life through meditation, the study of the *dharma*, and self-denial. His home is the *sangha*, as it was in the days of the Buddha. When a monk achieves the goal he is seeking, he attains *nirvana* and thus release from the cycle of birth, death, and rebirth. The laity studies the masters of meditation, but few can embrace the demanding discipline of the monastics. Thus most lay practitioners follow the Three Jewels (the Buddha, *dharma*, and *sangha*) and give alms.

Mahayana Buddhism 'The Greater Vehicle'

About two hundred years following the Buddha's death, certain subtle changes began to occur in the practice of Buddhism. A new direction of thought and practice developed which led to the formation of Mahayana Buddhism (perhaps 56% of all Buddhists). A main principle that developed was that Gautama was really more than a man. In contrast to the teachings of early Buddhism and those of the Theravada school, the Mahayanists regarded the Buddha as a universal principle, raised to almost theistic status. New writings (*sutras*) were formed, expanding the understanding of the *sangha*, the ideal, and the Buddha. It was asserted that one is called not just to individual liberation but to 'Buddhahood.'

Furthermore, the Mahayanists put forth that Gautama was not the only Buddha to whom people could appeal. If Gautama was an eternal being who had come to earth to help people, the Mahayanists maintained that there must be many others. The Mahayana teaching is that there are many Buddhas located in different parts of the cosmos, all of whom are capable of helping people on the path to enlightenment.

One subset of the Mahayana branch of Buddhism is *Zen*. Zen is the Japanese name for the school of Buddhism that has most stressed mental conditioning and meditation. It dismisses scriptures in favor of training for direct intuition of cosmic unity known as the 'Void.' Through meditation alone can a person come to Truth. The aim of Zen practice is enlightenment, or *satori*. One directly experiences the unity of all existence, often in a sudden recognition that nothing is separate from oneself. All aspects of life become at the same time utterly precious and utterly empty. This can only be experienced; it cannot be understood intellectually.

Tibetan Buddhism

A much later development in Buddhism came to be known as Tibetan or Tantric Buddhism (perhaps 6% of all Buddhists). Buddhism was introduced into Tibet around 630AD. In this expression of Buddhism, meditation engages both the mind and the senses with the use of *mantras* (chants used in worship), *mudras* (hand gestures used in worship), and *mandalas* (geometric patterns used in worship). The Tibetans do not see their path as distinctive in its goal. Its originality lies in its practices, which enable one to reach nirvana in a single lifetime, using spiritual and physical means (body, speech, vision, gestures). The spiritual and temporal leader of Tibetan Buddhists is the Dalai Lama. The current Dalai Lama was identified as the reincarnation of the 13th Dalai Lama in 1937 when he was two years old. He was formally installed as the 14th Dalai Lama in 1939. Since China's invasion of Tibet in 1959, the Dalai Lama has lived in exile in nearby Dharamsala, India. He continues to travel around the world in an effort to keep the voice of Tibet alive.

AN ORTHODOX PERSPECTIVE OF BUDDHISM

Theism vs. Non-theism

Buddhism is often described as a non-theistic religion. There is no personal God who creates everything and to whom prayers can be directed. The Buddhists at the 1993 Chicago Parliament of the World's Religions found it necessary to explain to people of other religions that they do not worship Buddha:

> The Buddha, founder of Buddhism, was not God or a god. He was a human being who attained full Enlightenment through meditation and showed us the path of spiritual awakening and freedom. Therefore, Buddhism is not a religion of God. Buddhism is a religion of wisdom, enlightenment, and compassion. Like the worshippers of God who believe that salvation is available to all through confession of sin and a life of prayer, we Buddhists believe that salvation and enlightenment are available to all through removal of defilement and delusion and a life of meditation.

Furthermore, a close reading of early Buddhist writings indicate clearly that the Buddha opposed authority, ritual, tradition, written scriptures, speculation about creation and God. He preached intense self-effort.

One of the fundamental aspects that set Orthodox Christianity apart from Buddhism is that there is the belief of a Creator God, a God who is transcendent, personal, and holy. Furthermore, Orthodoxy states that God, first introduced in the Hebrew Scriptures, came to earth in the form of a human in order to bridge this chasm between the human and the divine:

"God so loved the world that He sent His only Son, that whoever believes in Him will not perish but have eternal life."

—John 3:16

"God became man so that man could become God-like."

—St. Athanasius

While the Buddha taught self-effort, Christianity would introduce the term *synergy*. This word implies that for growth and fulfillment to manifest, both human effort together with God's grace are necessary. This may not result in fifty-percent human effort and fifty-percent God's grace. Instead, there is the understanding of a mutual, ongoing, dynamic relationship that all humans are invited to participate in. Buddhism states that ultimate reality is an impersonal Void or Emptiness. Christianity would counter by emphasizing that salvation and ultimate meaning result from this personal relationship with God, in the person of Jesus Christ.

Sin vs. Karma

One of the strong points that Buddhism and Christianity have in common is the emphasis on living a moral and ethical life. The Buddha's Eightfold Path of Liberation clearly outlines proper conduct, especially the moral concepts to refrain from:

1) the taking of life
2) stealing
3) immoral sexual behavior
4) lying
5) the taking of intoxicants

Certainly, the life of Jesus affirms the need to live a moral and ethical life. He offered many teachings on this theme, including the 'Golden Rule,' but also modeled proper conduct throughout his earthly life.

The difference, however, between Buddhism and Christianity regarding morality and ethics is in what the consequence are for breaking such guidelines. In Buddhism, we earlier established the term *karma*, which is defined as deserved pleasure or pain based on one's thoughts and deeds. The result of negative *karma* is continuing the cycle of life unabated, precluding entrance into the state of *nirvana*.

In Orthodox spirituality, the consequence for not living the prescribed guidelines of morals and ethics is the severing of one's relationship with God. What is at stake here is not simply the breaking of a 'rule,' but the breaking down of a holy relationship with the Giver of Life. What must be made clear is that this severing is unilateral, with the human person choosing to cut ties with God, not the reverse.

Another aspect of *karma* and sin that deserves attention is the role of suffering, a key concept within Buddhism. The Buddha would state that one suffers because of desires that cannot be eliminated. One Christian response to that supposition is that one suffers because of the consequences of sin: "the wages of sin is death" (Romans 6:23), meaning spiritual death because of our separating ourselves from God. We also suffer because, being made in the image of God, we are fulfilled only when we are in a relationship with God. Living outside that relationship brings about suffering on many levels: physical, psychological, emotional, and spiritual.

Another dimension where Buddhism and Orthodox Christianity share common ground is in the area of desires or passions, which often lead to karma and sin. Both religions relate to how desires or passions can lead to suffering and sin. But where Buddhism sets out to eliminate desires completely, Orthodoxy seeks not to destroy but to re-direct desires and passions toward God. St. Maximus the Confessor writes, "The soul is made perfect when its powers of passion have been completely directed towards God." Thus the passions are to be purified, not eradicated; transfigured, not eliminated.

In his excellent book, *Philokalia: The Bible of Orthodox Spirituality*, Anthony Coniaris writes:

> By God's grace the passions can be turned into virtues: pride can become humility; lust can become agape, the sacrificial love that God has for us; anger can become righteous indignation against evil; greed can become generosity; unfaithfulness can become steadfast; envy can become "rejoicing with those who rejoice;" sloth can become diligence – all this can be accomplished by God's grace and our cooperation with His grace through askesis, prayer, and vigilance.

The Community vs. The Individual

As stated earlier, one of the Three Jewels that the Buddha left his followers was the *sangha*, the community of monks and nuns. While the emphasis may seem to be communal, the Buddha also stated repeatedly that only through one's own efforts could one reach nirvana; no God, no saints, no intercessions. Simply meditation, discipline, and self-effort are required.

The cornerstone of the Christian faith is to be a member of the Body of Christ. The communal nature of the Church was realized from Apostolic times. On the day of Pentecost, the Holy Spirit unified the Apostles into one body. The Nicene Creed states clearly that the Baptized and Chrismated Christian is a member of the "One, Holy, Catholic, and Apostolic Church." To this present day, when a person is Baptized and Chrismated into the Orthodox Church, they are not being sanctified as *individuals*, but are being integrated into the Body of Christ, the Church.

How important is this communal connection with Christ and the Church? Listen to these words by St. John of Kronstadt, a nineteenth century Russian priest:

> Your soul seeks true life and its natural food. The food of the mind is truth; the food of the heart is peace and blessedness; the food of the will is lawfulness. Go to the Church; she will give you all this in plenty, for she possesses it superabundantly. She is the pillar and ground of the truth, because in her is the Word of God, manifesting the origin of all things – the origin of the human race, how man was created after the image and likeness of God, how he fell, and has been restored through the Redeemer of mankind; in her also is revealed the means of salvation, faith, hope, and love. She affords us peace and blessedness, through her divine service, above all through the sacraments. She teaches us the true way which leads to eternal life.

Prayer vs. Meditation

Early Buddhist monastics were taught to meditate on the *dharma*, the teachings of the Buddha. By meditating on the Four Noble Truths and the Noble Eightfold Path of liberation, together with discipline and self-effort, one could achieve nirvana. Achaan Chah, a contemporary Buddhist from Thailand, offers this reflection:

> Try to be mindful and let things take their natural course. Then your mind will become still in any surroundings, like a clear forest pool. All kinds of wonderful, rare, animals will come to drink at the pool, and you will clearly see the nature of all

things. You will see many strange and wonderful things come and go, but you will be still. This is the happiness of the Buddha.

One of the themes that emerge from this passage is the need for silence in the meditative process. This thought is also confirmed in the Book of Psalms, "Be still and know that I am God" (Psalm 46:10). There are other spiritual giants in the Christian tradition who encourage stillness in times of meditation. St. Basil the Great writes, "Stillness initiates the soul's purification." St. Thalassios the Libyan states: "Blessed stillness gives birth to blessed children: self-control, love, and pure prayer."

Perhaps that final point by St. Thalassios is what differentiates Buddhist meditation and Christian meditation. While being still is a starting point for Christians, the true goal of this process is *prayer*; dialogue and communication with the living God. Being still is a prelude, an introduction to prayer. But ultimately, the Christian seeks union and communion with God in prayer.

KEY TERMS

Buddha – Translated as 'The Enlightened One,' it also refers to the name of Siddhartha Gautama, the founder of Buddhism.

Dharma - In Buddhism, it refers to the teachings or truths concerning the ultimate order of things.

Dukkha – The suffering that is an inescapable aspect of human life, both physical and psychological.

Karma – The law that a person's thoughts and deeds are followed eventually by deserved pleasure or pain.

Mahayana – A school of Buddhism that arose about two hundred years after the Buddha's death. Translated as 'The Greater Vehicle,' it pays more attention to the spiritual needs of the laity.

Nirvana – The state of being free of egocentrism and the suffering that it causes. In positive terms, it is joy and peace.

Sangha – The community of Buddhist monks and nuns.

Tanha – In Buddhism, it is the thirst or craving that leads to suffering. In the second Noble Truth, it is identified as the cause of suffering.

Theravada – A school of Buddhism that is the older, more monastic expression of this religion. Translated as 'The Teaching of the Elders,' Theravadans imitate the Buddha's ascetic life to attain enlightenment.

Zen – A school of Buddhism that stresses mental conditioning and meditation. This method dismisses written scriptures in favor of discipline, silence, obedience, and direct experience.

SELECT WRITINGS IN BUDDHISM

Excerpts Attributed to Buddha:
To refrain from evil,
To achieve the good,
To purify one's own mind,
This is the teaching of all Awakened Ones.

You must be your own lamps, be your own refuges… Hold firm to the truth as a lamp and refuge and do not look for refuge to anything besides yourselves. A monk becomes his own lamp by continually looking on his body, feelings, perceptions, moods, and ideas in such a manner that he conquers the cravings and depressions of ordinary persons and is always diligent, self-possessed, and collected in mind. Whoever among my monks does this, either now or when I am dead, if he is anxious to learn, will reach the summit.

It is good to tame the mind, which is difficult to hold in and flighty, rushing about; a tamed mind brings happiness.

Do not go upon what has been acquired by repeated hearing; nor upon tradition; nor upon rumor; nor upon what is in a scripture; nor upon the consideration, 'the monk is our teacher'…When you yourselves know, enter on and abide in them.

Some children were playing beside a river. They made castles of sand, and each child defended his castle and said, 'this one is mine.' They kept their castles separate and would not allow any mistakes about which was whose. When the castles were all finished, one child kicked over someone else's castle and completely destroyed it. The owner of the castle flew into a rage, pulled the other child's hair, struck him with his fist and bawled out, 'He has spoiled my castle! Come along all of you and help me to punish him as he deserves.' The others came to his help. They beat the child with a stick and then stamped on him as he lay on the ground …Then they went on playing in their sand castles, each saying, 'this is mine; no one else may have it. Keep away! Don't touch my castle!' But evening came; it was getting dark and they all thought they ought to be going home. No one now cared what became of his castle. One child stamped on his, another pushed his over with both his hands. Then they turned away and went back, each to his home.

(on nirvana)

There exists something in which there is neither earth nor water, fire nor air. It is not the sphere of infinite space, nor the sphere of infinite consciousness, nor the sphere of nothingness. It is neither this world nor another world, nor both, neither sun nor moon. I do not state that it comes nor it goes. It neither abides nor passes away. It is not caused, established, arisen, supported. It is the end of suffering. What I call selfless is difficult to perceive, for it is not easy to perceive the truth. But one who knows it cuts through craving, and for one who knows it, there is nothing to hold onto. When there is no desire, there is neither coming nor going, and when there is no coming or going, there is neither death nor rebirth. When there is neither death nor rebirth, there is neither this life nor the next life, nor anything in between. It is the end of suffering.

QUESTIONS FOR REFLECTION

1) How would you compare the persons of Jesus and Buddha? What roles did they play in their respective traditions?

2) Does Buddhism fall into the category of philosophy or religion?

3) The Orthodox Christian faith emphasizes the heart as the center of one's being. Buddhism sees liberation through the mind. Do you tend to be a 'heart' person or a 'mind' person?

4) How does the Buddhist understanding of *nirvana* differ from the Orthodox understanding of salvation?

5) How does the Buddhist method of overcoming suffering (and healing) compare with the Orthodox Christian approach?

JAINISM

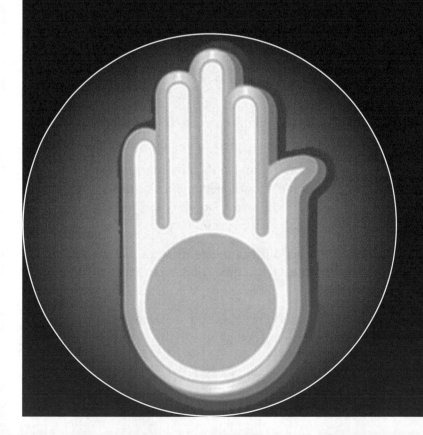

JAINISM IN HISTORY

850-800BC   Life of Parshva, the legendary twenty-third
tirthankara

599-527   Life of Mahavira, the twenty-fourth and
most recent *tirthankara*

350   Split between *Digambara* and *Shvetambara*
sects

1970AD   Jain monks establish Jain centers outside
India

JAINISM

The essence of right conduct is not to injure
anyone; one should know only this, that non-injury
is religion.

—Jainist Sutra

A careful reading of this survey on world religions makes
clear that India is the home of several major faiths, and quite
a few lesser known religions as well. Jainism falls into the
latter category. Although Jainists number less that four
million in the world, interest in this faith is reviving because
of its high standards of personal and social ethics, together
with its environmental sensibilities.

Practicing Jainists are viewed as uncompromising,
thought-provoking, noble, and even extreme. For example,
Jainism rejects warfare of any kind, or the killing of animals
for any reason. Jain teachings recognize that humans are
imperfect, but that through strict control of one's senses
and thoughts one can attain perfection, freedom, and
happiness.

Jainism evolved as a protest against Hinduism about
2500 years ago. Although Jainism does not technically

have a founder, followers often point to *Mahavira* ('great hero') as its major teacher. Mahavira was a contemporary of the Buddha, a prince of a wealthy family who renounced his position at the age of thirty to wander as a spiritual seeker. After twelve years of meditation, silence, and fasting, Mahavira claimed to have achieved liberation and perfection. For the next thirty years, he spread his teachings to 14,000 monks, 36,000 nuns, and 400,000 lay followers.

Following Mahavira's death, his teachings were not written down because the monastics lived as ascetics without possessions; they were initially carried orally by memory. Two hundred years later, Jain written texts were established into a canon of 45 books.

MAIN TEACHINGS OF JAINISM

The philosophical worldview of Jainism is dualistic – there is soul and matter. The soul, termed *jiva*, is life, eternal and valuable. Matter, on the other hand, is understood as lifeless, material, and evil. All persons are seen as soul encased in matter. The goal for persons practicing Jainism is to discover the soul's own perfect, unchanging nature and thus transcend the miseries of earthly life. This process may require many incarnations until finally being free from *samsara* (the wheel of birth, death, and rebirth). The gradual process by which the soul learns to extricate itself from the lower self and its attachments to the material world involve purifying one's ethical life until nothing remains but the purity of the *jiva*. One who achieves this status is called a *jina* (a 'winner' over passions).

Like Hindus and Buddhists, Jainists believe in *karma*, that our actions influence the future course of our current life, and our lives to come. But in Jain belief, karma is actually subtle matter – minute particles that accumulate as we act and think. Mahavira likened karma to coats of clay that weighs down the soul. Jainists are very careful to avoid accumulating karma. Three of the chief principles to which they adapt their lives to avoid karma are non-violence, non-attachment, and non-absolutism. These are the three ethical pillars of Jainism.

Non-Violence (Ahimsa)

This ethical pillar is the most dominant and well known aspect of Jainism. Jainists believe that every centimeter of the universe is filled with living beings, some of them minute. Humans have no special right to supremacy; all living things deserve to live and evolve as they can. To kill any living being has negative karmic effects. Jainists are not only vegetarians, but pursue occupations that avoid any possibility of harming living creatures, such as agriculture, the military, exterminators, or butchers. Instead, Jainists aspire to work in vocations such as banking, education, law, and publishing. *Ahimsa* also extends to care in speaking and thinking, for abusive words and negative thoughts can injure others as well.

Non-Attachment (Aparigraha)

Attachments to and love for other persons or things is one of the elements that keep humans bound to life. Possessions possess us; their acquisition and loss drive our emotions. It was for this reason that Mahavira renounced his family and possessions and refused to stay in any place longer than one day, lest he form new attachments. Non-acquisitiveness is considered the way to inner peace. If a person can let go of attachments, moment by moment, one can be free. The classic Jain story on this theme is as follows:

> There was once a monk who saw twelve stray dogs chasing another dog who was racing away with a bone he had found. When they caught the dog, they attacked him to get the prize. Wounded and

bleeding, he let go of it. The others immediately abandoned him to chase the one who picked up the bone. The monk saw the scene as a moral lesson: so long as we cling to things, we have to bleed for them. When we let them go, we will be left in peace.

Aparigraha is of value to the world community as well. Contemporary Jainists point out that their principle of limiting consumption offers a way out of the global poverty and hunger that result from unequal distribution of resources.

Non-Absolutism (Anekantwad)

This term is sometimes translated as 'relativity.' Jainists try to avoid anger and judgmentalism, remaining open-minded by remembering that any issue can be seen from many angles. Another Jain parable may help to clarify this ethical pillar:

A group of blind people were asked to describe an elephant. The one who felt the trunk said that an elephant is like a tree branch. The one grasping a leg argued that an elephant is like a pillar. The one grasping the tail insisted that an elephant is like a rope. And the one who encountered the side of the elephant argued that the others were wrong; an elephant is like a wall. Each had a partial grasp of the truth.

Jainists do not deny that there is some truth in the doctrines of other philosophies and religions. However, a philosophy or religion that claims any sort of absolute truth would be rejected. To Jainists, statements depend on time, place, and circumstances for the truth they contain, since times change, places change, and circumstances change.

Alexander Goussetis

SPIRITUAL PRACTICES

Jainism is traditionally an ascetic path and thus is practiced in its fullest by monks and nuns. In addition to the three pillars, monastics adopt a life of meditation, celibacy, and fasting.

Within ornate Jain temples, revered teachers are honored through images. Mahavira is the last of twenty-four *Tirthankaras* (bridge builders) who forged a bridge between this life and the 'ideal.' Images are venerated without expectation of a personal response to their prayers or help for the worshippers. One Jain teacher writes:

> In Jainism, unlike Christianity, there is no such thing as a heavenly father watching over us. To the contrary, love for a personal god would be an attachment that could only bind Jainists more securely to the cycle of rebirth. It is a thing that must be rooted out.

JAIN SECTS

In 350BC, Jainists were severely divided over what was to be the true meaning of Jainism, and they split into two sects that exist today. The sect that interprets Jain teachings more liberally is the *Svetambara*, literally 'the white clad.' They are liberal in their interpretation of Mahavira's teachings regarding the wearing of clothing and permit white garments to be worn.

The second sect, the *Digambara*, literally 'the sky clad,' is the more conservative of the two. They adhere to the traditional ideals and require that monks go about nearly nude. Women are prohibited from entering monasteries and temples. Because of its high regard for celibacy, it also rejects the tradition that Mahavira was ever married.

AN ORTHODOX PERSPECTIVE OF JAINISM

On the surface, Orthodox Christianity and Jainism appear to have very little in common. The Orthodox faith recognizes a deity; God as the Creator of all things visible and invisible. Jainists view the world through the lens of dualism; that matter is evil, that the soul is trapped inside the human body. Orthodoxy would also reject the understanding of reincarnation, instead viewing each human life as a unique and unrepeatable creation. Finally, Orthodoxy would rule out the Jainist call for non-absolutism, believing that relativism leads to distortion and syncretism.

There are, however, two fields within Jainism and Orthodoxy, that if not compatible, at least move towards a common interest. The first is the Jainist ideal of non-attachment, and the second is the ethical pillar labeled non-violence. The remainder of this chapter will address an Orthodox response to these Jainist terms.

Non-Attachment vs. Apatheia

Orthodox spirituality defines the 'passions' as any disordered appetite or longing that takes possession of one's soul: anger, jealously, gluttony, avarice, lust for power, pride, etc. Through watchfulness and diligence, Christians are called to battle against the passions in what is called unseen warfare.

Kallistos Ware, in his book, *The Orthodox Way*, highlights that passions are dynamic impulses originally placed in the human person by God, and so are fundamentally good, although at present distorted by sin:

> Our aim is not to eliminate the passions but to redirect their energy. Uncontrolled rage must be turned into righteous indignation, spiteful jealousy into zeal for the truth, sexual lust into an *eros* that is pure in its fervor. The passions, then are to be

purified, not killed; to be educated, not eradicated; to be used positively, not negatively. To ourselves and to others, we say, not 'suppress', but 'transfigure.'

The practicing Christian combats the passions using the tools of the faith: prayer, fasting, reading Scripture, attending worship services, participating in the sacramental life of the Church, reading the lives of saints, acts of charity, and other pieces of wisdom that the Church extends to the faithful.

This discipline, together with God's grace, results in *apatheia*, defined as 'the absence of passions.' More specifically, apatheia means that "...we are no longer dominated by selfishness and uncontrolled desire, but now become capable of true love. The dispassioned person, far from being apathetic, is the one whose heart burns with love for God, for other humans, for every living creature" (Kallistos Ware). Generally speaking, while Jainism's goal is to extinguish passions, Christianity strives to purify and transform them.

Non-Violence (Ahimsa) in a Fallen World

Violence, in general, and warfare in particular, has been a complex issue about which the Church has struggled with for many centuries. In the history of the Christian Church there have been three main approaches to war and military action. On one end of the debate are some Church Fathers, the pacifists who emphasize the words and deeds of Jesus and passages from Scripture that focus on the ideal of peace and peaceful living. Their position is that warfare is never an option.

In the middle ground are those who maintain the ideal of peace, but acknowledge that we live in a fallen world in which evil people need to be constrained. The Church Fathers in this group see war as a necessary evil, but certainly not the ideal. Generally speaking, this has been the mainline position of the historic Church.

Third, there have been periods in history when war was glorified as good and desirable. The chief example is the period of the Crusades encouraged by the Western church to free the Holy Land in the 11th and 12th centuries. This position has always been rejected by the Orthodox Church.

Let us focus our attention on the first two approaches to violence and war, beginning with the pacifist position. Before the time of Emperor Constantine in the 4th century, the pacifist position was clearly dominant. Many Church Fathers stated very strongly that killing in any form be rejected by Christians. St. Athenagoras wrote, "The seal of baptism and the seal of military service are incompatible." St. Cyprian of Carthage made this searing commentary: "If murder is committed privately, it is considered a crime. But if it happens with the authority of the state, they call it courage."

The early Church felt this strongly about violence and war because of the example and teachings that Jesus offered. In the New Testament the most important ethical teaching is love. Jesus taught to turn the other cheek, to avoid retaliation, to pray for enemies. In the Sermon on the Mount, Jesus proclaimed, "Blessed are the peacemakers." Given this attention to love, patience, and forgiveness emphasized in Scripture, it would be difficult to find an activity that is more at odds with the spirit of the Gospel than war.

Following the conversion of Constantine in 308AD, many Church writers began to take a middle ground on the issue of violence and war. Christianity became the religion of Byzantium, a 'Christian nation' responsible for protecting its people from marauders and external attacks.

While the Church Fathers of this era continued to see war as evil, they also recognized the importance of the role of the state to use military force to protect society and ensure the safety of its citizens. St. Ambrose wrote: "If a man fighting for personal gain deserves condemnation, that same individual is in quite a different position when he risks his life for the welfare of his country." One can summarize from the writings of this era that a Christian has the right to defend the lives of people in a society, even if it means the taking of a life in order to safeguard the innocent against unjustified attack.

One important qualifying statement should be offered here. St. Basil writes in one of his canons of the Church: a penance of three years abstinence from Holy Eucharist was recommended for those who kill in war. Perhaps this was a reminder of our ultimate goal as Christians; that our true citizenship is in heaven, not in any worldly nation.

A thoughtful and balanced summary statement on this topic is offered by Stanley Harakas, in his book, *The Orthodox Church: 455 Questions and Answers*:

> It may be necessary that wars be fought. It may be necessary that revolutions be waged. No matter how much we may want peace, it may not be possible to maintain it if our neighbor is intent on war. But war can never be our goal. It can only be a falling away from our goal for which repentance is the only appropriate response. In practice, Christians should always strive to be peacemakers, seeking to make peace a priority.

KEY TERMS

Ahimsa – The Sanskrit word that is translated 'nonviolence.' In Jainism, it is a reverence for all living things.

Anekantwad – The Sanskrit word that is translated 'non-absolutism.'

Aparigraha – The Sanskrit word that is translated 'non-attachment.'

Digambaras – The Jainists who follow the tradition that allows monks to wear clothes.

Jina – A person in Jainism who has conquered one's passions.

Jiva – Spirit or soul which enlivens matter.

Shvetambaras – The Jainists who believe that a true monk is 'sky clad,' meaning that they wear no clothing.

Tirthankara – The Sanskrit word that is translated 'bridge-builders'; the twenty-four founders of Jainism; they forged the bridge between life and Nirvana. The last of the Tirthankaras was Mahariva.

SELECT WRITINGS IN JAINISM

All breathing, existing, living, sentient creatures should not be slain, nor treated with violence, nor abused, nor tormented, nor driven away. This is the pure, unchangeable, eternal law …Correctly understanding the law, one should arrive at indifference for the impressions of the senses, and not act on the motives of the world.

All beings with two, three, four, or five senses…in fact all creation, know individually pleasure and displeasure, pain, terror, and sorrow. All are full of fears which come from all directions. And yet there exists people who would cause greater pain to them…Some kill animals for sacrifice, some for their skin, flesh, blood, feather, tusks,…some kill them intentionally and some unintentionally; some kill because they have been previously injured by them. He who harms animals has not understood or renounced deeds of sin…He who understands the nature of sin against animals is called a true sage who understands karma.

Difficult to conquer is oneself; but when that is conquered, everything is conquered.

Just as a fire quickly reduces decayed wood to ashes, so does an aspirant who is totally absorbed in the inner self and completely unattached to all external objects shake to the roots, attenuate, and whither away his karma-body.

Some foolish men declare that a Creator made the world. The doctrine that the world was created is ill-advised, and should be rejected.

If God created the world, where was he before creation? If you say that he was transcendent then, and needed no support, where is he now?

No single being had the skill to make this world – for how can an immaterial god create that which is material?

Know that the world is uncreated, as time itself is, without beginning and end.

A person who is emotionally attached to relatives or friends is a fool who will suffer greatly, because the numbers of those to whom one is attached always increase. Wealth and relatives cannot protect one from suffering. Only by understanding this and the nature of life will a person overcome karma.

QUESTIONS FOR REFLECTION

1) How would a person who practices Jainism reconcile the contradiction of no creator (or no god) and yet have ultimate respect for creation?

2) Of the three Jain ethical pillars, which is easiest for you to practice in your daily life? Which is the most difficult?

3) Of the three religions in India covered in this survey (Hinduism, Buddhism, Jainism), which is most compatible with Orthodox Christianity? Which is the most incompatible? Support your response with specific examples.

4) Monasticism plays a vital role in the practice of many religions in India? What role does monasticism play in Orthodox Christianity?

5) What are the advantages and disadvantages of forming separate states for peoples of different religions?

CONFUCIANISM

CONFUCIANISM IN HISTORY

551-479BC	Life of Kung Fu-tsu (Confucius)
372-289	Life of Mencius, interpreter and propagator of Confucius thought
221-206	Chin Dynasty – Confucian scholars suppressed, books burned
206BC-220AD	Confucian Classics used as a basis of civil service exams
630AD	All provinces in China ordered to conduct services in honor of Confucius
1130-1200	Life of Ju Xi, leading Neo-Confucius thinker
1900	Boxer Rebellion in China
1949	Communist Victory in China, led by Mao Zedong; Red Book replaces Confucian Classics
1966-1976	'The Cultural Revolution' in China; Confucianism suppressed
1990's	Confucian Classic reintroduced in schools

CONFUCIANISM

I am a transmitter, not an innovator; I believe in antiquity and have a passion for the ancients.
—Words Attributed to Confucius

Confucianism, like Taoism, is interwoven into the total philosophy of the Chinese people. Scholars contend that the teachings of Confucius and his followers were never intended to be a religion. In all likelihood, Confucius was an agnostic whose main concern was a just and orderly human society. If Confucianism is a religion, it is a very unique expression of one:

1) It has no clergy or priesthood.
2) Its sacred writings, although important, have never been considered a divine revelation like the Bible or the Quran.
3) It frowns upon asceticism and monasticism.
4) It has no doctrine of an afterlife, although the existence of a 'heaven' is not denied.

Troubled by what he perceived as a decline in civilization, Confucius advocated a program of comprehensive education and the cultivation of special virtues. He wanted both to develop individuals who could be social leaders and to create a harmonious society. He appealed to tradition and the past as a model for the present. In Confucianism thinking, to a great extent human beings are their relationships. Thus careful attention to the duties and obligations of a person's different relationships with others was central focus. One must live up to the highest expectations or standards of the various social roles one occupied, beginning with the family.

THE LIFE OF CONFUCIUS

Confucius was born in 551BC in what is now Shantung, China. At the time of his birth, China was not a single empire but a group of small kingdoms. His family name was Kung; the Chinese have honored him as Kung Fu-tsu (Kung the Master). The name has been westernized into Confucius.

Confucius was the child of an aristocratic family that had lost its wealth and position through political struggles. His family had been prominent in a previous dynasty. His father died when Confucius was a child. His mother was left to raise the boy alone. Despite his poverty, Confucius became a lover of literature, art, music, archery, and traditional Chinese social rituals. Although he aspired to be a scholar, the family's financial straits necessitated his taking such humble work as overseeing granaries and livestock. He married at the age of nineteen and had at least two children.

When he was twenty-three, Confucius' mother died, sending him into a three year mourning period. During this time he lived ascetically and studied ancient ceremonial rites (known as *li*). When he returned to social interaction, Confucius gained some renown as a teacher of *li* and of the arts of governing.

Because he lived during a time of political instability, Confucius felt that a return to classical rites and standards of virtue was the only way out of the chaos, and he earnestly but unsuccessfully sought rulers who would adopt his ideas. Confucius turned to a different approach: the training of young men to be wise and altruistic public servants. He believed that training rulers to be of high moral character, and visibly so, would inspire the common people to be virtuous.

He thus revived and instructed his students in the Five Classics of China's cultural heritage: poetry, history, rituals, music, dance, and the Spring and Autumn Festival of events. His edited collection of material is now known as the Confucian Classics. Of his role, Confucius claimed only: "I am a transmitter, not an innovator; I believe in antiquity, and have a passion for the ancients."

Confucius' work and teachings were considered relatively insignificant during his lifetime. After his death in 479 BC, interstate warfare increased, ancient family loyalties were replaced by large and impersonal armies, and personal virtues were replaced by laws and state control.

It was not until about 200BC that the Confucian Classics became influential, becoming the basis of civil servant examinations for those who would serve in the government. The life of a 'gentleman scholar' became the highest professed ideal. Eventually temples were devoted to the worship of Confucius himself as the model of unselfish public service, human kindness, and scholarship.

THE TEACHINGS OF CONFUCIUS

Foremost among the virtues that Confucius felt could serve society was *jen*. Translations of this central term include innate goodness, benevolence, and humaneness. This is a person who:

1) is not motivated by personal profit but by what is moral.
2) is concerned with self-improvement rather than public recognition.
3) speaks cautiously but acts quickly.
4) regards human nature as basically good.

The prime example of *jen* should be the ruler; ruling not with brute force but by personal virtue:

> Confucius said, "If a ruler himself is upright, all will go well without orders. But if he himself is not upright, even though he gives orders they will not be obeyed…One who governs with virtue is comparable to the polar star, which remains in its place while all the stars turn towards it."

The great need in every society, according to Confucius, is a model human being – a person who will set an example for others to follow. Confucius called his model person *junzi*. It has been translated as Superior Person or Mature Person. The *junzi* is opposite of the narrow-minded, selfish, petty, or aggressive person. The two are contrasted in the following passages from the *Analects* (sayings and dialogues of Confucius):

The *junzi* understands what is moral. The small person understands what is profitable.

The *junzi* agrees with others without being an echo. The small person echoes without being in agreement.

The *junzi* is at ease without being arrogant. The small person is arrogant without being at ease.

The Chinese concept of *li* is defined as the principle of harmony that should rule the home, society, and the empire. Words associated with *li* are appropriateness, protocol, etiquette, and conformity. According to Confucius, there are five basic relationships in life. If *li* were present in these relationships throughout society, the social order would be ideal. The five relationships are as follows:

1) **Father to son** – there should be kindness in the father and filial piety in the son.
2) **Elder brother to younger brother** – there should be gentility in the elder brother and humility in the younger.
3) **Husband to wife** – there should be righteous behavior in the husband and obedience in the wife.
4) **Elder to junior** – there should be consideration among the elders and deference among the juniors.
5) **Ruler to subject** – there should be benevolence among the rulers and loyalty among the subjects.

All five are asymmetrical relationships in that behavior that is appropriate to one person in each pair differs from what is appropriate for the partner. On the surface, the one person has 'power' or 'influence' over the other person. Confucius taught that authority should not be lorded over the 'weaker' partner. The key to harmony in the five relationships is the following statement: *Li* is the outward expression of the superior (mature) person toward society. The inward expression of the relationship is *jen*.

Briefly, a final term associated with Confucius thought is *Te*. Basically it defines the style by which a society is ruled. The Realists, a group of thinkers during Confucius' time, were lead by brute force. Confucius would say that *Te* should be the power of moral example.

CONFUCIANISM AFTER CONFUCIUS

Confucianism did not dissolve into a myriad of divisions or branches like Buddhism or Christianity. A number of personalities after Confucius added their own nuances to Confucius' thoughts over the next 2500 years, including Mencius in 300BC and a Neo-Confucius period around 1200AD. In addition, Confucianism has been fused with various forms of Buddhism, Taoism, and Chinese folk religion over these past 2500 years.

The most severe criticism of Confucianism came in the twentieth century when Mao Zedong formed the People's Republic of China in 1949. Communism replaced Confucianism, with Mao attempting to transform society through secular means. During the Cultural Revolution (1966-1976), Confucianism was attacked as one of the 'Four Olds' – old ideas, culture, customs, and habits. Although Confucius thought was officially abandoned, its fundamental doctrines continued in respect to Chinese family values and ethical life. In the 1990's, a revival of sorts began when Confucius teachings were reintroduced into Chinese schools.

AN ORTHODOX PERSPECTIVE OF CONFUCIANISM

Ethics vs. Religion

Before the time of Confucius, folk religion played a major role in the life of the Chinese people. Folk religion offered an integration, or recognition, of heaven and earth. Heaven (*Ti* or *Tien*) was presided over by God (*Shang Ti*). The emphasis was on one's continuing relationship with one's ancestors. Those on earth offered sacrifices to their ancestors, who, in return offered guidance for their future (in the form of signs). The practitioners of folk religion perceived that their ancestors were transcendent figures who were seen as living somewhere close to God; thus the emphasis was on heaven.

Confucius reversed this emphasis, without removing heaven from the picture. When the issue of heaven was broached, he would simply return the conversation to the present; in short, one world at a time. Attention was shifted from ancestor worship to present relationships and our duty in the here and now.

Although Confucius did not elaborate on the understanding of God, nor did he deny the existence of God, he did believe in a power that emphasized a moral compass. His emphasis was on duties of the living rather than speculation about life after death. In summary, Confucianism does not emphasize the continuation of the person in a transcendent life in heaven. Instead, it is the continuation of the person's ethical influence on the thoughts and values of his or her descendents.

From an Orthodox Christian perspective, Confucianism's emphasis on a strong moral and ethical life is applauded. The role of a *junzi* in Confucianism is certainly compatible with the spiritual father or mother in Orthodoxy. However, Orthodoxy would stress that ethics come about as a result of one's dogmatic beliefs. The foundation would first be the establishment of doctrine; then would follow the ethical application of the doctrine, which is the moral and ethical life.

Using Orthodox terminology, the Nicene Creed is an example of the establishment of certain non-negotiable beliefs or dogma. The Canons of the Church are the moral and ethical application which best expresses the basic doctrines of the faith. This is why the Church Canons may change over time; the application of the faith needs to fit into the context of one attempting to live the Orthodox faith.

Orthodoxy also would quibble with the understanding of ancestor worship in Chinese folk religion. Certainly the Church offers countless opportunities for memorial prayers and remembrance of the dead. Furthermore, Orthodoxy encourages seeking the prayers and intercessions of the Saints of the Church. But to emphasize that God and one's ancestors only provide a moral compass would be seen as limited from an Orthodox viewpoint. The basis of the Christian faith is establishing a relationship with the living God, and seeking union and communion with God throughout this life and into the next. The focus of this relationship is first based on love, followed by the moral and ethical expectations that come with being a Christian.

Five Classics vs. Tradition

Confucius stressed the riches of China's history, including rites and rituals, music, dancing, and poetry. He believed that reintroducing, or reemphasizing, these jewels would restore order and perspective; the past can give guidance for the future. The Orthodox Christian faith is also renowned for its recognizing the influence of the past. One term that is frequently highlighted is 'Apostolic Succession,' which accentuates the unbreakable link to the people, places, and events that have shaped Orthodoxy from the time of Christ to the present.

Perhaps a contemporary Orthodox Christian, using the approach of Confucius, could illustrate the jewels of our faith history. Could an argument be made that the 'Five Classics' of Orthodoxy are Scripture, Sacraments, iconography, the liturgical cycle of services, and the writings of the Church Fathers and Mothers? The point is that Orthodoxy treasures the contributions of our past in order to cultivate holiness and perspective for present and future Orthodox Christians.

The Greater Good

From an Orthodox Christian viewpoint, Confucius' accentuation of the entire body of a community is compatible with Scripture and the writings of the Church saints. Confucianism is not an individualistic belief system but is concerned with the whole organism. He placed great importance in the five basic relationships, the building blocks of a society. Even the asymmetrical aspects of these relationships underline humility and respect for the 'weaker' members of a society. For a Christian exegesis of this theme, Paul writes about the Body of Christ in 1 Corinthians 12:

> For just as the body is one and has many members, and all the members of the body, though many, are one body, so it is with Christ…The parts of the body which seem to be weaker are indispensable, and those parts of the body which we think less honorable we invest with greater honor…Now you are the body of Christ and individually members of it.

This theme of the greater good can even be extended to the responsibility that each of us has to influence others towards the Christian path. In the Gospel of Matthew, Jesus states, "Let your light so shine before others, that they may see your good works, and glorify your Father who is in heaven" (Mt 5:16). St. John Chrysostom writes an excellent pericope on the need to be a good example:

> Christ left us here to be lights. We are here to teach others and be like leaven in dough. In this way they can profit as we become seeds bearing copious fruit. There is no need to speak if we shine through our lives. There is no need for teachers if we only demonstrate through our works. There would be no unbelievers if we were the Christians we should be.

Jen vs Phronema

Both Confucianism and Orthodox Christianity agree that the human person is by nature good. The viewpoint of the 'depravity of man,' found in some Protestant circles and especially in Calvinist theology, is absent here. A disciple of Confucius, Mencius, upholds this basic goodness and states that man's free will at times leads to unfortunate consequences:

> Man's nature is naturally good just as water naturally flows downward. There is no man without this good nature; neither is there water that does not flow downward. Now you can strike water and cause it to splash upward over your forehead, and by damming it, you can force it uphill. Is this the nature of water?

Orthodox Christianity clearly states that the greatest gift that God has given to us is life. The second greatest gift extended to humankind is free will, the ability to choose. The goal in Confucianism is to develop this free will to the point of *jen*; innate goodness, benevolence, and humaneness. The Orthodox companion to *jen* might be the term *phronema*, which means one who imbues the spirit of Orthodoxy in every aspect of one's daily life. Every thought, every behavior, every decision is based on the perspective of Jesus and the Christian framework.

KEY TERMS

Analects – A collection of sayings and dialogues attributed to Confucius.

Five Classics – A corpus of texts considered authoritative by the early Confucians. They include poetry, history, rituals, music, dance, and cultural events.

Jen – Translations of this central term include innate goodness, benevolence, and humaneness.

Junzi – Confucian term for a person of high moral character.

Li – Originally referred to ritual and correct conduct in society; later understood as the Confucian principle of protocol, ritual, and propriety.

Mandate from Heaven – Refers to the natural law or moral order within things.

Te – The style by which a society is ruled. Confucius would say that Te should be the power of moral example.

Tian – Term for heaven or god in the first millennium before Christ, when Confucius lived.

SELECT WRITINGS IN CONFUCIANISM

The Master said, "He who by reanimating the Old can gain knowledge of the New is fit to be a teacher."

The Master said, "As to being a Divine Sage or even a Good Man, far be it from me to make any such claim. As for unwearying effort to learn and unflagging patience in teaching others, those are merits I do not hesitate to claim."

I have no hopes of meeting a sage. I would be content if I met someone who is a gentleman.

Our central self or moral being is the great basis of existence, and harmony or moral order is the universal law in the world.

To find the central clue to our moral being which unites us to the universal order, that indeed is the highest human attainment.

The Master said, "Put your words into action before allowing your words to follow your action."

(On Jen)
One who is free to choose, yet does not prefer to dwell among the Good – how can he be accorded the name wise?

(On Jen)
Without goodness a person cannot endure adversity, cannot for long enjoy prosperity.

(On Junzi)
The good person does not grieve that other people do not recognize her merits. Her only anxiety is lest she should fail to recognize theirs.

(On Junzi)
A noble mind can see a question from all sides without bias. Small minds are biased and see a question only from one side.

(On Junzi)
The noble person can influence those who are above her; the small person can only influence those who are below her.

Someone said to Confucius, "Why do you not take part in government?" The Master said, "*The Book of History* says, 'Simply by being a good son and friendly to his brothers a man can exert an influence upon government.' In so doing a man is, in fact, taking part in government. How can there be any question of his having actively to 'take part in government'?"

QUESTIONS FOR REFLECTION

1) Is Confucianism a religion, an ethic, or a humanistic philosophy?

2) Is the Confucian hierarchical view of relationships viable in the modern era?

3) Which of the 'classical' elements of the Orthodox faith are you most inspired by: Scripture, Sacraments, iconography, the liturgical cycle of services, or the writings of the Fathers and Mothers of the Church? Which area would you like to learn more about?

4) Is Confucianism too much tied to Chinese culture to be transferable to another culture?

5) Can society be changed for the better by educating leaders and role models in the arts?

TAOISM

TAOISM IN HISTORY

600-500BC	Legendary life of Lao Tzu
365-290	Life of Chuang Tzu, Taoist writer
100AD	Taoist immortality movements begin
600-900	Mutual influences between Taoism and Buddhism
748	Taoist Canon first compiled
960	Tai-Chi appears
1900	Boxer Rebellion in China
1911	Last imperial dynasty overthrown
1949	Communist Victory in China, led by Mao Zedong
1966-1976	'The Cultural Revolution' in China; Taoism suppressed
1990's	Taoist sects & temples re-established

TAOISM

The wise person chooses to be last and so becomes the first of all.

—Lao Tzu

Taoism is extremely difficult to define. It does not have a clearly articulated set of doctrines or practices such as Christianity or Islam. Instead, Taoism embodies observations about nature, philosophical insights, guidelines for living, exercises for health, and practices for attaining longevity and inner purity.

Confucianism and Taoism share many common traits and influences, since they both evolved within the boundaries of China. These include:

1) similar historical timelines.
2) similar cultural influences, including *li* (rituals and social conduct).
3) similar effects from indigenous religions, including: ancestor worship, the great spiritual being of Shang Ti, the Mandate of Heaven.
4) similar effects of communism in the 20th century.

From the ancient roots of China gradually developed two contrasting ways of harmonizing with the cosmos – the more mystical religious ways which are collectively called Taoism, and the more political, social, and moral ways known as Confucianism. Taoism argues that the natural course of things is the best; left undisturbed, the natural course leads to harmony and perfection. Artificial structures among persons or in society, meaning culture or elaborate government, eventually bring discord. A philosophy of nature, a religion, a system of magical practices – Taoism is all of these.

HISTORICAL DEVELOPMENT

The beginnings of Taoism are somewhat obscure. The origins of the *Tao Te Ching* (translated as *The Way and Its Power*), a book attributed to Lao Tzu, founder of Taoism, is disputed. Speculations about Lao Tzu's life have inspired many legends. Was he an elderly sage who left a deep impression on the young Confucius? Did the two masters ever meet? Scholars do not agree on an answer. Some believe that Lao Tzu lived during the 6th century BC. Others prefer a later date, perhaps in the fourth, third, or even second centuries BC.

One legend states that Lao Tzu was the keeper of royal archives in the court of the Chou dynasty. Tired of the artificial life in court, he retired and journeyed westward where he sought to leave the country. The guard recognized the wise man and refused to allow him to leave until he had committed to writing the sum of his wisdom. Thereupon, Lao Tzu sat down and wrote the *Tao Te Ching*. When this was completed he was allowed to leave, and was never seen again. The truth of this story has never been verified. Certainly we know less about the founder of Taoism than we know about any of the founders of world religions.

The *Tao Te Ching* is a small book, made up of slightly more than five thousand words contained in eighty-one chapters, and is usually translated into poetic form. Some scholars believe that the book was developed over many centuries. Arthur Waley, author of *The Way and Its Power* (George Allen & Unwin, 1956), suggests that the book was written as a polemic against the Confucians who wished for a strong central government. Taoism emphasizes or values the solitary individual rather than the Confucian idea of an organized society. Put in other words, Taoism emphasizes one's private life, philosophy, and meditation, while Confucianism idealizes government and family life.

MAIN TEACHINGS OF EARLY TAOISM

The beliefs of the early Taoists are difficult to piece together. The two main sources for the seminal days of Taoism are the *Tao Te Ching* and the work of Lao Tzu's disciple named Chuang Tzu. The teachings of early Taoism centers around the following themes:

1) **Behind the universe is a mysterious and undefinable force called the Tao.**
Tao is a mysterious thing; it's beyond knowing, beyond description, and beyond identification.

Though the Tao is defined as 'the way,' it is most often compared to a stream or a moving body of water as it progresses endlessly.

The universe arises from the interplay of *yin* and *yang*. They are modes of energy commonly represented as interlocking shapes, with dominance continually shifting between the dark, receptive *yin* mode and the bright, assertive *yang* mode. Wisdom lies in recognizing their ever-shifting, but regular and balanced, patterns and moving with them.

Yin	**Yang**
Passive	Active
Cold	Hot
Dark	Light
Death	Life
Weak	Strong
Responsive	Aggressive
Negative	Positive

Those who insist on their own way or who force society into their own plan may seem to succeed for a while, but inevitably the pendulum will swing the other way.

2) **Wu-Wei** (pronounced *woo-way*)

Wu-wei is the principle of accomplishing tasks without aggression. Individuals in harmony with the flow of the Tao can accomplish more than individuals who assert themselves. For example, water may seem the most pliable or unresisting element in the world. Yet over time it can wear down even mountains of the most solid rock.

Another example of *wu-wei* is a ruler who gets others to do his will by silent example or subtle persuasion. In general, *we-wei* is a deliberate removing of one's hands from something and letting nature, or the Tao, take its course.

3) **Life is to be lived simply**.
The early Taoists believed that life itself was the greatest possession. Fame, wealth, power, and education were transient illusions, or worse yet, impediments to living. Ideally, individuals should turn their backs on the advancements of civilizations and live as simply and as quietly as possible.

According to early Taoist philosophers, the least government is the best government. Lao Tzu is remembered for saying, "govern a nation as you would cook a small fish – do not overdo it." The small unit is the ideal unit of society. The best ruler is the one who rules least and is virtually anonymous.

4) **Little theism or speculative thought**
There is very little theism in early Taoism. The Tao itself is an impersonal, vague force behind the universe and is more of a First Cause than a god in any traditional sense of the word. In one translation of the *Tao Te Ching*, the word *god* is used only once; in many translations it does not appear at all. Only rarely does the word *heaven* appear.

The Tao is not understood as a force to whom one can pray or sacrifice to, and the early Taoists seem to have had no rituals for worship. In all the early Taoist writings, the sage talks *about* the Tao, never *to* the Tao.

The early Taoists also seem to have little concern for life after death. In general, they were concerned about the quality of life as it is lived on a day-to-day basis, without much interest in the heavens, the gods, rituals, or life after death.

LATER DEVELOPMENTS IN TAOISM

Basically, early Taoism as it is seen in the Tao Te Ching and in the essays of Chuang Tzu was concerned with living life in harmony with the basic force behind nature. Following the period of the early Taoist philosophers, two kinds of Taoists developed. One group followed the philosophical writings of Lao Tzu and Chuang Tzu. The second group, which developed around 100AD, was searching for immortality, not in the sense of life after death, but an endless extension of the present life through various means. Long life appealed to the Chinese, who looked forward to old age and the relative ease and honor that it had traditionally brought in Chinese culture.

This large and diverse sect of Taoism is characterized by belief in many gods and ancestral spirits, magic, superstition, ritual, the use of priests, and even meditation and special dietary regulations. Many scholars believe that this sect of Taoism was heavily influenced by Chinese folk religions and Mahayana Buddhists.

One of the practices of this sect of Taoism includes *alchemy*, usually a term meant to describe a process of transforming base elements into gold. For Taoists, alchemy is defined as finding elixirs of immortality. Some believe that ingesting gold could lead to immortality, since gold does not tarnish or decay.

Another practice of this sect, familiar to Westerners, is *Tai-Chi. Chi* is often translated as vital life force. *Tai-Chi* is a body-centered practice which looks like slow swimming in the air, with continual circular movement through a series of dance-like postures.

AN ORTHODOX PERSPECTIVE OF TAOISM

Relational God vs. Impersonal Force

How do Orthodox Christians and Taoists understand the nature of God? The one area of common ground between the two faiths is the appreciation of the mystical component of God. However, Orthodoxy would go to great lengths to emphasize the two ways to understand the nature of God – the unknown yet well known, the hidden yet revealed. Orthodox tradition draws a distinction between the *essence*, nature or inner being of God, on the one hand, and his *energies*, operations or acts of power, on the other.

St. Athanasius writes, "God is outside of all things according to his essence, but he is in all things through his acts of power." St. Basil writes, "We know the essence through the energy. No one has ever seen the essence of God, but we believe in the essence because we experience the energy."

Bishop Kallistos Ware, in his classic book, *The Orthodox Way*, comments:

> The essence signifies the radical transcendence of God; the energies, his immanence and omnipresence…By virtue of this distinction between the divine essence and the divine energies, we are able to affirm the possibility of a direct or mystical union between man and God – what the Greek Fathers term the *theosis* of man.

Ware continues that God is beyond and above all that we can think or express, yet closer to us than our own heart.

Why is this distinction between God's essence and energies so important to understanding the Christian life? Because Christianity is more than belief in an almighty higher power; it encourages an ongoing and living relationship with a knowable God. This relational dynamic is highlighted in these two excerpts from Alexander Elchaninov's book, *The Diary of a Russian Priest*:

> We do good deeds, purify our heart and draw nearer to God, not in order to obtain a reward but out of love for God. One day I asked myself: would I remain with Christ if I knew for certain that the devil will defeat God? And I answered without hesitation: of course I would remain with Him.

> What matters in prayer is our act of turning consciously to God, our humility, the feeling of connection and dependence; and besides this, there is the importance of framing things explicitly in words, of communion (with God).

Many of the world religions stress the importance of living a moral and ethical life. The Orthodox faith, of course, also emphasizes morality and ethical behavior. But to emphasize ethics *at the expense* of experiencing the mystery of God would not be compatible with the Christian faith. The Church has a greater role than simply teaching ethics.

In the book *The Mountain of Silence*, author Kyriacos Markides writes about his ongoing dialogue with Father Maximos, a monastic cleric in Cyprus. Consider the perspective that Father Maximos offers regarding the person of Christ in the life of the Church (or *Ecclesia*):

> "People are confused. They think that the aim of our existence is primarily to become good human beings, or to become moral, socially well-adjusted, and well-balanced personalities."

> "I thought becoming good is what the *Ecclesia* is all about," replied Markides.

"No, not only that. This pietistic notion is not the essential purpose of the *Ecclesia*. It is a gross misconception. What the *Ecclesia* primarily teaches is the means through which a human soul may attain *Christification*, its saintliness, its union with God. The ultimate goal is to become perfect in the same way as our Heavenly Father is perfect, to become one with God. Christ didn't come into the world to teach us how to become good fellows, how to behave properly, or how to live a righteous life in this world…He came to the world to give us Himself."

Wu-wei vs. Servant Leadership

From an Orthodox Christian perspective, the Taoist application of *wu-wei* in relationships is intriguing. As highlighted earlier, *wu-wei* is the principle of accomplishing tasks without assertion.

In the New Testament, one can find numerous examples of Jesus' leadership style while displaying elements of *wu-wei*. Following the institution of the Last Supper, Jesus knelt down and washed the disciples' feet, emphasizing that servant leadership is the Christian norm. On another occasion, James and John, the sons of Zebedee, were discussing greatness. Jesus reminds them:

You know that those who are supposed to rule over the Gentiles lord it over them, and their great leaders exercise authority over them. But it shall not be so among you; but whoever would be great among you must be a servant, and whoever would be first among you must be servant of all. For the Son of Man also came not to be served but to serve (Mark 10:42-45).

Many Christians find themselves in a position of power, whether at home, at work, or at Church. The goal should be to strive, as Jesus models, to serve others rather than dominate or manipulate the power that has been given to us. The proper stewardship of the divine power that God gives always builds up our fellow human beings. St. Nilus of Ancyra reminds us, "One should teach through deeds; anyone who does not do this proves that he holds leadership not for the good of others, but for his own gratification."

Mystery vs. Magic

Taoism took a strange turn about six hundred years after its genesis. As highlighted earlier, variations of Mahayana Buddhism and Chinese folk religion led to the formation of a new expression of Taoism. Magic, superstition, and alchemy were a few of the supernatural ingredients that flourished into a new sect within Taoism.

From an academic Western perspective, Orthodoxy certainly uses a number of non-rational approaches in applying the faith in everyday life. Water is blessed "for the drinking and sanctification of our souls and bodies" (Theophany service); oil is blessed for the anointing and healing of souls and bodies; bread and wine are consecrated and transformed into the Eucharist; icons are seen as physical manifestations of holiness; relics of saints are reverenced by the faithful, to name a few. Even the Western term *sacrament* is replaced by the word *mysterion*, or mystery, in Orthodoxy.

Yet, Father Maximos, quoted in the book *The Mountain of Silence*, makes clear that superstition is quite different from mystery:

> Many people consider him (Fr. Maximos) to be some
> kind of magician. "They came here at the monastery
> to find out whether someone cast a spell on them,
> why they were abandoned by their lover or their

husband and so on. At first I couldn't figure out why they would come to me with such problems. Then I realized that they thought of me as some kind of sorcerer capable of undoing spells."

"What do you tell them in such cases?" (asked Markides).

"I tell them there is no magic to resolve their problems; that they need to do spiritual work. I tell them that if they have a problem with demonic energies then they can follow the prescriptions of the *Ecclesia* to heal themselves: confession, participation in the mysteries, fasting, charity, prayer, and *askesis* in general. That's the way to do it."

"But are they receptive?" (asked Markides)

"Hardly. Most people crave a quick fix. They are too lazy or unwilling to invest any effort of their own. They assume if I read some magic formula over their heads, their problems will disappear...Of course, some do follow the therapeutic guidelines of the *Ecclesia* and see results."

Creator vs. Creation

Taoists believe that nature always existed; that it was not created. Furthermore, by living close to nature and studying its ways, humans can learn to remain healthy and wise.

The Nicene Creed makes vividly clear what Christians believe. Stated in the very first verse, "I believe in one God, the Father Almighty, Creator of heaven and earth . . ." Orthodoxy undeniably claims that there is a distinction between the Creator and creation. That nature was created by the will of God; that creation was therefore a free, gratuitous act of God.

Following the creation of things visible and invisible, God, in the book of Genesis, reminds us to have dominion over the earth, to preserve and cultivate creation (Genesis 1:28). In Psalm 24, the author writes, "The earth is the Lord's, and the fullness thereof; the world and everything that dwells therein." In this verse Christians recognize that God is the creator of nature and we humans are called to nurture, protect and care for His creation.

(For a more developed Orthodox view of nature, please refer to the "Orthodox Perspective" section under the Jainism heading.)

KEY TERMS

Alchemy – In Taoism, it is defined as finding elixirs of immortality.

Dao/Tao – The Chinese word for 'way'. For Taoist, the idea is both descriptive of the dynamic flow of nature and prescriptive for a naturalness to be implemented in human affairs.

Tai-Chi – In Taoism, it is the concept that underlies breathing and exercise routines.

Wu-wei – Non-action, the preferred Taoist path of least resistance, allowing things to run their natural course.

Yang – The Chinese principle of nature that is positive, life, aggressive, and masculine.

Yin – the Chinese principle of nature that is negative, death, passive, and feminine.

SELECT WRITINGS IN TAOISM

The Tao that can be told is not the eternal Tao. The name that can be named is not the eternal Name. The namable is the eternally real. Naming is the origin of all particular things. Free from desire, you realize the mystery. Caught in desire, you see only the manifestations.

The Tao is like a well: used but never used up. It is like the eternal void: filled with infinite possibilities. It is hidden but always present. I don't know who gave birth to it. It is older than God.

The Tao is infinite, eternal. Why is it eternal? It was never born; thus it can never die. Why is it infinite? It has no desires for itself; thus it is present for all beings.

There was something formless and perfect before the universe was born. It is serene. Empty. Solitary. Unchanging. Infinite. Eternally present. It is the mother of the universe. For lack of a better name, I call it the Tao.

It flows through all things, inside and outside, and returns to the origin of all things.

Man follows the earth. Earth follows the universe. The universe follows Tao. The Tao follows only itself.

Empty your mind of all thoughts. Let your heart be at peace. Watch the turmoil of beings, but contemplate their return. Each separate being in the universe returns to the common source. Returning to the source is serenity.

Those who know don't talk. Those who talk don't know. Close your mouth, block off your senses, blunt your sharpness, untie your knots, soften your glare, settle your dust. This is the primary identity.

Practice not-doing, and everything will fall into place.

Fill your bowl to the brim and it will spill. Keep sharpening your knife and it will blunt. Chase after money and security and your heart will never unclench. Care about people's approval and you will be their prisoner…Do your work, then step back; the only path to serenity.

Being and non-being create each other. Difficult and easy support each other. Long and short define each other. High and low depend on each other. Before and after follow each other.

The Tao doesn't take sides; it gives birth to both good and evil.

Throw away holiness and wisdom and people will be a hundred times happier. Throw away morality and justice, and people will do the right thing. Throw away industry and profit, and there won't be any thieves.

Nothing under heaven is softer or more yielding than water; but when it attacks things hard and resistant there is not one of them that can prevail. For they can find no way of altering it. That the yielding conquers the resistant and the soft conquers the hard is a fact known to all people, yet utilized by none.

QUESTIONS FOR REFLECTION

1) What are the strengths and/or weaknesses of the Taoist term *wu-wei*? Did Jesus practice a system similar to *wu-wei*? Explain.

2) Does my personality type lean towards the *yin* or *yang* mode? How does this affect my life?

3) What other differences/similarities do you see between Orthodox Christianity and Taoism? What are the main differences between Taoism and Confucianism?

4) What role does mystery play in your life and faith? Do you prefer the rational and dogmatic aspects of Orthodoxy or the dimension of mystery in the faith?

5) In studying any religion, what period of its history/ teachings should be emphasized: its initial roots or 1000 years later?

JUDAISM

JUDAISM IN HISTORY

2000BC	Abraham, the first Patriarch, establishes covenant with God
1250	Exodus of the Hebrews from Egypt, led by Moses
1000-965	Establishment of Jerusalem as the capital of the Israelite kingdom by King David
950	Completion of the First Temple by Solomon
721	End of northern kingdom, destroyed by Assyria
586	First Temple destroyed; Jews exiled to Babylon
515	Dedication of the Second Temple
430	Torah established
200	Completion of the last books of the Hebrew Scriptures
70AD	Destruction of the Second Temple of Jerusalem by Romans
90	Hebrew Scriptures formed into canon
200	Rabbis complete the Mishnah
480	Rabbis complete the Talmud
1135-1204	Life of philosopher Moses Maimonides
1480-1492	The Inquisition begins; mass expulsion of Jews from Spain
1700's	Reform movement begins in Germany
1800's	Conservative movement begins in Germany

Alexander Goussetis

1937-1945	The Holocaust; destruction of much of European Judaism by the Nazis
1948	Beginning of Israel as an independent Jewish state
1950's	Reconstructionism movement led by American Mordecai Kaplan
1967	Six-Day War; Israel defeats enemies and expands its territory, holding Golan Heights, West Bank, Old City of Jerusalem, and Sinai
1979	Israel and Egypt, in cooperation with President Jimmy Carter, sign a peace treaty

JUDAISM

Hear, O Israel: The Lord our God is one Lord; and you shall love the Lord your God with all your heart, and with all your soul, and with all your might.

—Deuteronomy 6:4-5

Judaism is the smallest of the great world religions, comprising less than one-half of one percent of the world's population. Yet Jews have had, and continue to have, a major impact on history. Describing the religion of Judaism is made more complex by the fact that some Jews today do not consider themselves religious but do consider themselves Jewish. Further clouding the issue of defining a Jew occurred during the 1930's and 1940's when Adolph Hitler found it expedient to label Judaism in terms of race. Despite the variety of understanding the Jewish people in categories of religion, culture, and/or race, our focus here will be on the rudimentary teachings of Judaism.

A basic working definition of Judaism is a belief in the oneness of God who works in and through historical events and who has in some manner chosen the Jewish people as agents. Important in its own right, the study of Judaism is also needed to explain the development of both Christianity and Islam, which also worship the God of Abraham.

ABRAHAM AND THE BIBLICAL PATRIARCHS

Historically, Jews were a loose collection of semi-nomadic tribes that wandered in what is today Israel, Jordan, Lebanon, and Syria. The dramatic history of Judaism focuses on an encounter between God and Abraham. With Abraham, God took the initiative to intervene in human history. Around 2000BC, God communicated with Abraham, challenging him to emigrate to the land surrounding the Sea of Galilee and the Dead Sea, called Canaan:

> The Lord said to Abram, "Go forth from your native land and from your father's house to a land that I will show you. I will make of you a great nation, and I will bless you; I will make your name great, and you shall be a blessing."
>
> —Genesis 12:1-2

Abraham was promised that he would become the father of a great nation, possess a great land, and become a blessing to all people if he were faithful to his part of a covenant with God. Abraham is succeeded in this covenant by his son Isaac, his grandson Jacob (who is renamed Israel), and Jacob's twelve sons. These figures are called the patriarchs of the Jewish people because they are the physical forebears of the nation. Their stories are found in Genesis 12-50.

The Book of Genesis closes with a great nation springing up from the descendants of Abraham, but they were not in Canaan. They were in Egypt, where they were bound in slavery. Therefore, the exodus from Egypt to Canaan had to be accomplished before God's promise to Abraham could be fulfilled. The events and personalities of the Exodus became the heart and soul of the Jewish religion. God acted to save his chosen people, the Israelites, miraculously delivering them from slavery from the most powerful nation in the world (Egypt). These events are remembered annually in the various major holidays of Judaism.

The Book of Exodus opens with the Israelites crying out for deliverance from their enslavement by the Egyptians. The key figure in this drama of salvation is Moses. Endangered as an infant, Moses was rescued and raised by the daughter of the pharaoh of Egypt. After recognizing his Israelite heritage and killing an Egyptian in defense of a Jewish slave, Moses was exiled to the Sinai Desert, where he lived for forty years as a shepherd.

In the desert, the God of Abraham was revealed to Moses and spoke through a bush that was burning but was not consumed. God declared that his name was Yahweh and commanded Moses to lead the Israelites from their slavery. Moses returned to Egypt, and, after a series of ten miraculous plagues upon the Egyptians, was able to gain the release of the Israelites. When the Israelites fled Egypt, they were pursued by the pharaoh, who had changed his mind about their release. The waters of the Red Sea were parted by Yahweh, and the Israelites crossed through on dry land.

The next significant event was the giving of the law on Mt. Sinai. After crossing the Red Sea, the Israelites came to Mt. Sinai on their journey to Canaan. From this mountain, Yahweh communicated the law to the Israelites through Moses. Ten absolute laws that are basic to Jewish life are found in Exodus 20:1-17 and Deuteronomy 5:6-21. Basically these commandments stress obedience and loyalty to Yahweh and decent behavior toward members of the community. After a period of wandering in the desert, Moses' successor, Joshua, led the Israelites into Canaan.

Much of the remaining material found in the Hebrew Scriptures deals with a recurring cycle that occurs to the Israelite community. After a period of peace and prosperity, the Israelites would become lax in their loyalty to God. This laxity would be followed by an outside oppressor dominating the Jewish peoples. When persecuted, the Israelites would then cry out to God for safety and salvation, promising to remain faithful to the covenant. God would eventually redeem the Jewish people, and peace and prosperity would reign once again.

THE HEBREW SCRIPTURES

The Hebrew Scriptures were written in the Hebrew language, and partly Aramaic, over the course of one thousand years or more. The divinely inspired material in this collection of books tells the story of God's interaction with the Israelites from approximately 2000BC until the time of Jesus. It contains the creation account, God's covenant with the Israelites, (salvation) history over two thousand years, wisdom literature, and ultimately, God's promise to save humankind and the world through the 'Anointed One' (Messiah, Christ). The Hebrew Scriptures contain thirty-nine books, although the *Septuagint*, the Greek translation of the Hebrew Scriptures, contains forty-nine books.

This collection is divided into four sections:

1) **'Books of the Law' or Pentateuch**: Genesis, Exodus, Leviticus, Numbers, and Deuteronomy. These books describe God's creation of the world, the original rebellion and fall of humankind, and the initiation of the covenant between God and Israel from the time of Abraham (2000BC) to the time of Moses (1250BC). The material was compiled between the 10th-5th centuries before Christ. The Jews call this section the *Torah*, which is Hebrew for 'law'.

2) **'Books of History'**: Joshua, Judges, Ruth, Esther, etc. These books of history, which were written between the 12th century before Christ to the first century after Christ, trace the life of ancient Israel from the 13th century before Christ to the time of Jesus.

3) **'Books of Wisdom'**: Job, Psalms, Proverbs, etc. These books contain poetic, philosophical, and theological discourses which argue that happiness is possible only through faith in and obedience to God. The books of wisdom were compiled between the 11th-1st centuries before Christ.

4) **'Books of the Prophets'**: Isaiah, Jeremiah, Ezekiel, Daniel, etc. Most of these books were written between the 8th-4th centuries before Christ. Prophets were not fortunetellers who predicted the future. They were divinely inspired to announce God's will. They were outspoken in proclaiming right worship and social justice. Oftentimes they were persecuted because people rejected their message.

MAJOR THEMES IN EARLY JUDAISM

The One God

The central Jewish belief is monotheism. There is one Creator God, creator of all things visible and invisible. God is everywhere, as David sings in the Psalms:

Where can I escape from your spirit? Where can I flee from your presence? If I ascend to heaven, you are there; if I descend to Sheol, you are there too. If I take wing with the dawn to come to rest on the western horizon, even there your hand will be guiding me, your right hand will be guiding me fast.

—Psalm 139:7-14

In traditional Judaism, God is sometimes perceived as a loving Father who sometimes needs to chastise his children.

Love for God

The essential commandment for humans is to love God. The central prayer in any Jewish religious service is the *Shema* Israel:

> Hear, O Israel: The Lord our God is one Lord; and you shall love the Lord your God with all your heart, and with all your soul, and with all your might. Take to heart these instructions with which I charge you this day. Impress them upon your children. Recite them when you stay at home and when you are away, when you lie down and when you get up. Inscribe them on the doorposts of your house and on your gates.
>
> —Deuteronomy 6:4-9

One should not love God from selfish or fearful motivations, such as receiving earthly blessings or avoiding problems in the life after death. One should study the *Torah* and fulfill the commandments out of sheer love of God.

The Sacredness of Human Life

Humans are the pinnacle of creation, created in the image of God, according to the account of creation in Genesis 1. Jews do not take this passage to mean that God literally looks like a human. It is often interpreted in an ethical sense; endowed that they can mirror God's qualities such as justice, wisdom, righteousness, and love. Human life is sacred, rather than lowly or loathsome. The body and soul are an inseparable totality: "I praise you, for I am awesomely and wondrously made" (Psalm 139:14).

Law

Because of the great responsibility of humankind, traditional Jews give thanks that God has revealed in the *Torah* the laws by which they can be faithful to the divine will and fulfill the purposes of creation, in which all creatures can live in peace and fellowship. When Jews act according to the *Torah*, they feel they are upholding their part of the ancient covenant with God.

MAJOR BRANCHES TODAY

Orthodox

The Orthodox Jews stand by the Hebrew Bible as the revealed word of God and the Talmud as the legitimate oral law. Within this framework there are great individual differences, with no central authority or governing body. Orthodox Judaism includes mystics and rationalists, Zionists and anti-Zionists.

Reform

This branch of Judaism is at the other end of the religious spectrum from Orthodoxy. This movement began in the 18th century in Germany as an attempt to help modern Jews appreciate their religion rather than regarding it as antiquated or meaningless. Worship was modernized to include choirs and prayers eliminated references to animal sacrifices. Observances were reevaluated for their relevance to modern needs. Judaism was understood as an evolving, open-ended religion rather than one fixed forever by the revealed *Torah*.

Conservative

This intermediate position of Judaism is the largest movement in the United States. It arose in Germany in the 19th century as a response to Reform Judaism. While Conservative Jews feel they are totally dedicated to traditional rabbinical Judaism, at the same time they are restating and restructuring it in modern terms so that it is not perceived as a dead historical religion. They believe that Jews have always searched and added to the laws, liturgy, and beliefs to keep them relevant and meaningful in changing times. Some of the recent changes introduced are acceptance of riding to a synagogue for Sabbath services and acceptance of women into rabbinical schools as candidates for ordination as rabbis. These changes are not forced on local congregations, which have the right to accept or reject them.

Reconstructionism

Rabbi Mordecai Kaplan, an American who died in 1983, branched off from Conservatism and founded a movement called Reconstructionism. Kaplan held that Judaism needed to be protected from the extremes of rationalism. He defined Judaism as an "evolving religious civilization," both culturally and spiritually. Kaplan denied that the Jewish people were specially chosen by God. He created a new prayer book, deleting traditional portions such as derogatory references to women and Gentiles, and references to the physical resurrection of the body. Women were accepted fully into synagogue participation.

AN ORTHODOX PERSPECTIVE OF JUDAISM

Old Covenant vs. New Covenant

God's special relationship with ancient Israel was grounded upon the covenant with Abraham and his descendants. In the covenant, God promised his people deliverance from their enemies and a free, peaceful, and happy life in Canaan, the land of fulfillment. The promise was contingent upon Israel's fidelity and obedience to God. But ancient Israel, as the Hebrew Scriptures reveal, did not keep the terms of the covenant with God.

From a Christian perspective, the failure of the Israelites to live up to the covenant was part of the divine plan for the salvation of the world. The omniscient God of all creation foresaw that human means could never bridge the chasm between God and humankind.

In his book, *The Message of the Bible*, author George Cronk makes the following observation:

> Only in the perfect faith and obedience of the Messiah, Jesus Christ, would an Israelite measure up to the standards of the divine law. Only through the perfect and personal union of God and man in Jesus could the requirements of God's covenant with his people be met. The incarnation was necessary to the fulfillment of the covenant with Israel, because no man could perfectly obey the divine law unless God became man. And that, according to the Christian faith, is exactly what happened in Jesus Christ…In Christ, the old Israel is superseded by the Christian Church, the new Israel, the body of Christ; the old covenant is completed in the new covenant in and through Jesus Christ.

The ramifications of this new covenant are immense. Membership in Christ and this new covenant is now based upon faith, not upon genealogical lineage; the Church is an Israel of the spirit, and not of the flesh. The coming of this new covenant was alluded to by the Prophet Jeremiah:

> Behold the days are coming, says the Lord, when I will make a new covenant with the remnant of the house of Israel; not like the covenant which I made with their fathers when I took them by the hand to bring them out of the land of Egypt, my covenant which they broke. But this covenant …I will put

my law within them, and I will write it upon their hearts; and I will be their God, and they shall be my people.

—Jeremiah 31:31-34

Monotheism in Judaism and Christianity

From an Orthodox Christian perspective, the God of the Bible is a perfect, personal being, possessing all holiness, truth, goodness, joy, and power. In addition to these fundamental attributes of the divine nature, Orthodox biblical theology also holds that Holy Scripture reveals the Trinitarian being of God – one God, three persons. This is certainly true in the New Testament, where there are many references to the three persons of the Trinity.

There are, however, several places in the Hebrew Scripture where the tri-unity of God seems to manifest itself. The chief passages in the Old Testament which testify to the Trinity of God are as follows:

Genesis 1:1, and the following verses: the name of God, *Elohim*, in the Hebrew text has the grammatical form of the plural number.

Genesis 1:26: "And God said, let us make man in our own image, after our likeness." The plural number indicates that God is not one person.

Genesis 3:22: "And the Lord God said, Behold, Adam is become as one of us, to know good and evil." These are the words of God before the banishment from paradise.

Genesis 11:6-7: Prior to the confusion of tongues at the building of the tower of Babylon, the Lord said, "Let us go down, and there confound their language."

Genesis 18:1-3, concerning Abraham: "And the Lord appeared unto him at the oak of Mamre …and he (Abraham) lifted up his eyes and looked, and behold, three men stood by him …and he bowed himself toward the ground and said, My Lord, if now I have found favor in your sight, pass not away, I pray, from your servant."

In addition, many Fathers of the Church see an indirect reference to the Trinity in the following passages:

Numbers 6:24-26: The priestly blessing indicated by God through Moses is in a triple form: "The Lord bless you …The Lord make his face shine upon you …The Lord lift up his countenance upon you."

Isaiah 6:3: The doxology of the Seraphim who stand about the throne of God is in a triple form: "Holy, holy, holy, is the Lord of hosts."

Psalm 32:6: "By the word of the Lord were the heavens established, and all the might of them by the Spirit of His mouth."

Immortality of the Soul/Life after Death

The Hebrew Scriptures emphasize a good life on earth more than the joys of heaven. In early Judaism, there was a belief that souls of the departed slept in *Sheol*, but most people did not find that prospect attractive. The Pharisees, a Jewish sect in the first century, believed that the body is resurrected; the Sadducees, another Jewish sect in the first century, denied it. Judaism today avoids embalming bodies and uses plain wooden boxes that will decay after burial. In reading Jewish services, there is an absence of specific descriptions of life after death.

From an Orthodox Christian perspective, Jesus of Nazareth was (is) the Messiah, the Christ who did not reestablish an earthly kingdom of Israel, but inaugurated the heavenly kingdom of God, through His life, death, and resurrection. This God-man Christ, through His death and resurrection, liberated humankind from the tyranny of sin and death. Through faith in Christ as Lord and Savior, humankind can be reconciled with God and experience the life of the Trinity. While this message may constitute a stumbling block for Jews (and many others), it is, for the Christian, the very power and wisdom of God (1 Corinthians 1:24).

(For more on the theme of the resurrection of Jesus Christ, please refer to the "Orthodox Perspective" section under the heading of Hinduism.)

KEY TERMS

Covenant – In Judaism, it is a special bond created between God and Israel; chosen people called to holiness.

Diaspora – A Greek word for the dispersion of Jews; Jews who live outside the Holy Land.

Kabbalah – A Jewish mystical movement that flourished during the Middle Ages. Magical incantations, charms, interpretations of dreams, numerology have been connected under the heading of Kabbalah. Not highly regarded by mainstream Judaism, but defined here because of its recent popularity.

Messiah – The anointed king that Jews have awaited as their deliverer since the late biblical era. From a Christian perspective, Jews were anticipating an earthly leader on the model of David, not the person of Jesus.

Mishnah – Teachings of the rabbis compiled about 200AD. The Mishnah records discussions of rabbis on how best to best live according to the Torah.

Sabbath – A day Jews set aside for worship. Keeping a Sabbath means maintaining a fence against worldly preoccupations, limiting secularity. The Jewish Sabbath runs from sunset Friday until sunset Saturday night.

Talmud – The collection of rabbinic teachings (including the Mishnah). It has deep influence over the lives of Jews from the beginning of the medieval period to the present.

Zionism – The Jewish movement dedicated to the establishment of a politically viable Jewish state in the biblical land of Israel.

HOLY DAYS

Rosh Hashanah – The Jewish New Year, a time of spiritual renewal. It is a movable feast celebrated in the fall.

Yom Kippur – Follows ten days after Rosh Hashanah. It honors and renews the sacred covenant of the Jewish people with God, but it does so in the spirit of atonement. There is an attempt at personal inner cleansing; individuals ask pardon from everyone they may have wronged during the past year.

Sukkot – A fall harvest festival. A simple outdoor booth is built as a dwelling for seven days. The fragile home reminds the faithful that their real home is in God, who sheltered their ancestors (in tents) on the way from Egypt to the Promised Land.

Hanukkah – During the darkest time of the year is celebrated the Feast of Dedication. Each night for eight nights, a candle is lit on a special candleholder called a menorah. Hanukkah commemorates the rededication of the Jerusalem temple after the Maccabean revolt against the Syrians (164BC). According to tradition, when the Jews regained access to the temple, they found only one jar of oil left undefiled, only enough to stay lit for one day. But by a miracle, the oil remained burning for eight days.

Passover – A Jewish holiday in the Spring. It celebrates God's deliverance of the Hebrews from slavery in Egypt during the time of Moses. During the last of the ten plagues, in which all first-born Egyptian sons were to be killed, the Hebrew homes were 'passed over' without harm.

SELECT WRITINGS IN JUDAISM

In the beginning God created the heavens and the earth. The earth was without form and void, and darkness was upon the face of the deep; and the Spirit of God was moving over the face of the waters. And God said, "Let there be light"; and there was light. And God saw that the light was good; and God separated the light from the darkness. God called the light Day, and the darkness he called Night. And there was evening and there was morning, one day.

—Genesis 1:1-5

Then God said, "Let us make man in our image, after our likeness, and let them have dominion over the fish of the sea, and over the birds of the air, and over the cattle, and over all the earth, and over every creeping thing that creeps upon the earth." So God created man in his own image, in the image of God he created him; male and female he created them. And God blessed them, and God said to them, "Be fruitful and multiply, and fill the earth and subdue it."

—Genesis 1:26-28

"I am God Almighty, walk before me, and be blameless. And I will make my covenant between me and you, and will multiply you exceedingly." Then Abram fell on his face; and God said to him, "Behold, my covenant is with you, and you shall be the father of a multitude of nations…And I will establish my covenant between me and you and your descendants after you throughout their generations for an everlasting covenant, to be God to you and to your descendants after you. And I will give to you, and to your descendants after you, the land of your sojournings, all the land of Canaan, from an everlasting possession; and I will be their God."

—Genesis 17:1-8

And God spoke all these words, saying, "I am the Lord your God, who brought you out of the land of Egypt, out of the house of bondage. You shall have no other gods before me. You shall not make for yourself a graven image…You shall not take the name of the Lord your God in vain…Remember the Sabbath day, to keep it holy…Honor your father and your mother…You shall not kill. You shall not commit adultery. You shall not steal. You shall not bear false witness against your neighbor. You shall not covet your neighbor's wife."

—Exodus 20:1-17

The Lord is my shepherd, I shall not want. He makes me lie down in green pastures. He leads me beside still waters; he restores my soul. He leads me in paths of righteousness for his name's sake. Even though I walk through the valley of the shadow of death, I fear no evil; for you are with me; your rod and your staff they comfort me. You prepare a table in the presence of my enemies; you anoint my head with oil, my cup overflows. Surely goodness and mercy shall follow me all the days of my life; and I shall dwell in the house of the Lord forever.

—Psalm 23

In the latter time he will make glorious the way of the sea, the land beyond the Jordan …The people who walked in darkness have seen a great light; those who dwelt in a land of deep darkness, on them has light shined. Thou hast multiplied the nation, thou hast increased its joy…For to us a child is born, to us a son is given; and the government will be upon his shoulder, and his name will be called, 'Wonderful Counselor, Mighty God, Everlasting Father, Prince of Peace.'

—Isaiah 9:1-6

For I know the plans I have for you, says the Lord, plans for welfare and not for evil, to give you a future and a hope. Then you will call upon me and come and pray to me, and I will hear you. You will seek me and find me; when you seek me with all your heart, I will be found by you, says the Lord, and I will restore your fortunes and gather you from all the nations and all the places where I have driven you, says the Lord, and I will bring you back to the place from which I sent you into exile.

—Jeremiah 29:11-14

Alexander Goussetis

QUESTIONS FOR REFLECTION

1) Is Judaism a religion, a culture, a race, or something else?

2) What role should culture play in one's religious life?

3) Is the Hebrew covenant between God and ancient Israel still valid and operating? Why or why not?

4) What aspects of Judaism are still present in Orthodox faith and practice?

5) What are the main religious questions raised by the Holocaust?

ISLAM

ISLAM IN HISTORY

570	Birth of Muhammad
610	Muhammad receives first Quranic revelation
622	Muhammad's *hijrah* (migration from Mecca to Yathrib); first year of the Muslim lunar calendar
630	Muhammad gains control over Mecca
632	Death of Muhammad
636-641	Muslim conquest of Damascus, Jerusalem, Egypt, and Persia
750-1258	Height of Islamic civilization; patronage of art and culture, development of Islamic law, and rising trade, agriculture, industry, and commerce
1453	Constantinople falls to Ottoman Muslims
1947	Independence of Pakistan as a Muslim nation
1979	Ayatullah Khomeini rules Iran under Islamic law

ISLAM

There is no God but Allah and Muhammad is his messenger.

—The Shahadah

Islam is the last of the three monotheistic faiths that arose in the Middle East, coming after Judaism and Christianity. Though it is the youngest of the major world religions, Islam is also the second largest, with more than one billion adherents.

Muslims see Islam not as a new religion but as the fulfillment or continuation of Judaism and Christianity. Muslim belief joins the Jewish and Christian understanding of God's work: God created the world and Adam and Eve, and from them all peoples; God sent prophets such as Abraham, Moses, and David to guide humankind; and God worked through Mary and made her son Jesus a great prophet. The interpretations of these events are understood differently by Muslims, but the link to Judaism and Christianity must be made.

In Islamic theology, *Allah*, the Arabic word for 'the God,' chose to work through the person of Muhammad. Thus Muhammad was the spokesman, the medium of a definitive message and book, called the *Quran*. Through it God expressed once and for all his divine mercy and judgment.

BIOGRAPHY OF MUHAMMAD

Muhammad was born in 570AD in Mecca, which is in present day Saudi Arabia. At that time most of the people in the area lived in nomadic tribes, supporting themselves through trading caravans. Muhammad, translated as 'the praised one,' was born into a poor family. His father died before Muhammad was born, and his mother died while he was still a young boy. Muhammad was raised by his uncle, who put him to work as a shepherd. At the age of twenty-six, he married Khadijah, a woman fifteen years his senior. They had six children together, of which four girls survived.

Muhammad would spend periods of time in solitary retreat, not uncommon in his lineage. When he was forty, during one of his spiritual retreats, the angel Gabriel reportedly came to him, insisting that Muhammad recite a prayer. Three times Muhammad refused, claiming he was unlettered. Muhammad at last cried out, "What shall

I recite?" and the angel began to dictate the first words of what became the Quran:

> Proclaim in the name of the Lord who created
> Who created man of blood coagulated.
> Proclaim! The Lord is the most beneficent,
> Who taught by the pen,
> Taught man that which he knew not.
> —Quran 96:1-5

Muhammad returned home deeply shaken. Khadijah comforted him and encouraged him to overcome his fear of the responsibilities of prophethood. The revelations continued intermittently for the rest of Muhammad's life, asserting the theme that it was the One God who spoke and who called all people to Islam, which means 'complete trusting surrender to God.'

After three years of receiving revelations, Muhammad was instructed to preach publicly. He and his followers were ridiculed; converts were few in the early years of his ministry. The turning point came in the year 622 when pilgrims from Yathrib (later renamed Medina), a city 280 miles north of Mecca, recognized Muhammad as a prophet. They invited him to come to their city to help solve its social and political problems. This migration from Mecca to Medina, called *hijrah*, is so important in Muslim history that the year 622 is the year in which Muslims calculate the beginning of their calendar.

In Medina, Muhammad drew up a constitution of the city and served as an administrator. Hostilities and suspicions between Medina and Mecca grew to the point of open conflict. Although Muhammad was personally involved in this warfare for about ten years, he was also instrumental in negotiating a truce between these two warring cities. Muhammad died in the year 632. He left no clear instructions as to who should succeed him.

THE QURAN

The heart of Islam is not the Prophet Muhammad but the revelations he received. Collectively they are called the *Quran*, which is an Arabic word meaning 'reading' or 'reciting.' Muhammad, acting as a stenographer, received the messages directly from Allah over a period of twenty-two years. The Quran is divided into 114 chapters called *suras*. The entire text is somewhat smaller than the New Testament.

With the exception of a brief introductory statement, the text is arranged according to the length of the *suras*, in descending order. Therefore, the non-Muslim reader is sometimes confused because there is no topical or chronological arrangement of the material. The recitation of the Quran is to be rendered in what is described as a sad, subdued tone, because the messages concern God's sadness at the waywardness of the people. Muhammad is stated as saying, "Weep, therefore, when you recite it."

Muslims believe that the Jewish prophets and Jesus all brought the same messages from God. However, the *Quran* teaches that God's original messages have been distorted by humans. In the Muslim view, the *Quran* was sent as the final correct and authoritative message from God.

Muslims, citing John 14:26 from the New Testament, believe that Jesus prophesied the coming of Muhammad when he promised that the Paraclete or Advocate would come to assist humanity after him. Of course, Christians believe that Jesus was speaking about the Holy Spirit on the day of Pentecost.

THE FIVE PILLARS

Those things that one must do to be a good Muslim are usually referred to as the Five Pillars of Islam. These pillars, or obligations, are the foundations upon which Islam as a

Alexander Goussetis

religious system of faith and social responsibility, worship, and piety rests. Each of the Five Pillars has an outer and public dimension and an inner and private expression.

Repetition of the Shahadah

The most common religious act of the Muslim is the frequent repetition of the creed of Islam – "There is no God but Allah and Muhammad is his messenger." These are the first words a Muslim child hears and they are likely to be the last words uttered by a dying Muslim. The devout utter this statement as often as possible every day, and the mere utterance of it makes the reciter a Muslim.

Daily Prayer (Salat)

The second pillar is the performance of a continual round of daily prayers. Five times a day (dawn, noon, mid-afternoon, dusk, and two hours after sunset) the faithful are to perform a ritual cleansing with water, face Mecca, and recite a series of prayers and passages from the *Quran*, while bowing and kneeling. Around the world this joint facing of Mecca for prayer unites all Muslims into a single family. There may be an *Imam*, or prayer leader, but no clergy or intercessor stands between the worshipper and Allah. On Friday at noon there is usually a special service in the *mosque*, but Muslims observe no Sabbath day. There are no liturgical services and no sacraments, since nothing in this life could mediate divine enlightenment.

Almsgiving (Zakat)

At the end of the year, all Muslims must donate at least two and one-half percent of their income to needy Muslims. This provision is designed to help decrease inequalities in wealth and to prevent personal greed.

Fasting (Sawm)

Frequent fasts are recommended to Muslims, but the

only one that is obligatory is the fast during *Ramadan*, which commemorates the first revelations of the *Quran* to Muhammad. The fast of Ramadan requires a dawn-to-sunset abstention from food, drink, smoking, and sexual relations.

Pilgrimage (Hajj)

All Muslims who can possibly travel to Mecca are required to do so at least once in their lifetime. Once in Mecca, Muslims take part in a series of rituals designed to bring them close to Allah:

- Males wrap themselves in a special garment, like a burial shroud, for two reasons. First, such clothing emphasizes no class distinctions among the faithful. Second, by wearing a burial shroud, the shroud represents dying to earthly life and devoting oneself to God

- Pilgrims walk around the *Kabah* (a cubicle said to have been built by Abraham) seven times, like the continual rotation around Allah by the angels and all of creation, to the seventh heaven.

- In addition, pilgrims carry out other symbolic gestures, such as sacrificing animals and throwing stones at the devil, represented by pillars. The animal sacrifice reminds Muslims of Abraham's willingness to surrender to God that which was most near to him, his own son Isaac.

Along with these Five Pillars of Islam, Muslims follow an injunction called *jihad*. Basically, *jihad* is defined as a holy struggle; a warfare in defense or pursuit of a good cause. There are two means of expressing jihad:

- On the inner level, *jihad* means striving against the lower self. It is the internal fight between right and wrong, error and truth, selfishness and selflessness.

- On the external level, *jihad* is exerting effort to protect the 'Way of God' against the forces of evil.

This *jihad* is the safeguarding of the faith and integrity of the Muslim community.

DIVISIONS WITHIN ISLAM

The preceding information describes the beliefs of all Muslims, although varying interpretations of these beliefs have always existed. After Muhammad's death resentments over the issue of his succession began to divide the unity of the Muslim community into factions. The two main opposing groups have come to be known as the *Sunni*, who now compose about eighty percent of all Muslims worldwide, and the *Shiite*.

Sunni
- Insist that Muhammad's successor (or *caliph*) should be elected.
- Emphasize the authority of the written traditions, which include not only the *Quran* but also the *Sunna* (meaning 'custom', from which the *Sunnis* derive their name) which includes the *Hadith*. Another important document within Islam is the *Shariah*, which includes teachings and practices for everything in Muslim life, from how to conduct war to how to pray. The *Shariah* sets the pattern for all individual actions into a regulated and coherent system.
- More consensus-oriented in the application of the sacred writings into one's daily life.
- Believe there should be a separation between civil and religious authorities.

Shiite
- Believe that Muhammad's successor should come through Muhammad's bloodline. Rather than recognize the *Sunni* caliphs, *Shiites* pay

their allegiance to a succession of twelve *Imams*, legitimate hereditary successors to Muhammad. The twelfth *Imam* was commanded to go into a hidden state to continue to guide the people and return publicly at the Day of Resurrection (similar to the Second Coming of Christ). The source of authority was passed to the *Ulama*, clerical scholars who consider themselves collectively to be general representatives of the hidden *Imam*.

- More authority-oriented – the Ayatollah Khomeini of Iran, for example, was a *Shiite* leader.
- Believe that the religious authorities should exercise both political and religious power.

A third and lesser known branch of Islam is *Sufism*, the mystical wing. The goal of the *Sufi* is to renounce worldly attachments, live an ascetical and simple life, and to unite their souls with God. *Sufi* writers are known for short stories that focus on the presence of God in everyday life. In these stories, the poor man turns out to be rich, or the fool turns out to be truly wise.

As well, Sufi's question the rational 'right-brain' portion of the human person, arguing that the more intuitive, 'left-brain' aspect of a person must have its due if one is to achieve balance and fullness. Predictably, the Sufi's have often been rejected by fundamentalist Muslims for not following the letter of the law. These same critics also claim that Christian and Buddhist monastics have influenced *Sufi* thought, thus distorting the truth of the *Quran*.

AN ORTHODOX PERSPECTIVE OF ISLAM

Jesus as Prophet vs. Jesus as Savior

Without question, Islam and Christianity share many common theological ideas. Both religions trace their roots from the moment of creation, to the persons of Adam, Eve, and Noah, to the covenant with Abraham. A brief list of other similar bonds between the two faiths would include the following:

God is one (monotheistic)
God as creator of all
God as sovereign and omnipotent
God spoke to humanity through
    prophets, angels, and sacred written words
The reality of Evil
The reality of Angels
Prayer
Almsgiving
Fasting
Emphasis on missions
Life after death/judgment

Of course, the primary distinction between Islam and Christianity is in understanding the person and role of Jesus. For Muslims, Jesus is viewed and respected as a prophet and teacher, but it is scandalous for Muslims to consider Jesus as divine, or the Son of God. Muslims deny that God can 'beget' a son and consider the Christian belief in the Trinity as blasphemous polytheism.

Kenneth Cragg, a Christian who is a scholar of Islam, and the author of *Jesus and the Muslim*, offers the following observation:

Through all we have reviewed there runs a great tenderness for Jesus, yet a sharp dissociation from his Christian dimensions. Islam registers a profound attraction but condemns its Christian interpretation. Jesus is the theme at once of acknowledgement and disavowal. Islam finds his nativity miraculous but his Incarnation impossible. His teaching entails suffering but the one is not perfected in the other.

He is highly exalted, but by rescue rather than victory. He is vindicated but not by resurrection. His servanthood is understood to disclaim the sonship which is its secret. His word is scripturised into the incidence of the Quran fragmentarily. He does not pass as personality into a literature possessing him communally. Islam has for him a recognition moving within a non-recognition, a rejectionism on behalf of a deep and reverent esteem.

Simply stated from a Christian perspective, Jesus Christ is the Messiah, the expected Savior written about in the Hebrew Scriptures and affirmed by the Church through Scripture and Tradition. Scripturally, we learn about the person of Jesus Christ in the Prologue of the Gospel of John:

In the beginning was the Word, and the Word was with God, and the Word was God. He was in the beginning with God; all things were made through him, and without him was not anything made that was made…And the Word became flesh and dwelt among us, full of grace and truth; we have beheld his glory, glory as of the only Son from the Father
—John 1:1-4, 14

The affirmation of the personhood of Jesus Christ in Tradition is conveyed by the First Ecumenical Council in Nicaea, which produced this statement in the Nicene Creed:

And in one Lord, Jesus Christ, the only-begotten Son of God, begotten of the Father before all ages. Light of Light, true God of true God, begotten, not created, of one essence with the Father, through whom all things were made. For us and for our salvation, He came down from heaven and was incarnate by the Holy Spirit and the Virgin Mary and became man. He was crucified for us under Pontius Pilate, and He suffered and was buried. On the third day He rose according to the Scriptures. He ascended into heaven and is seated at the right hand of the Father. He will come again in glory to judge the living and the dead. His kingdom will have no end.

Based on the Scriptural and doctrinal understanding of Jesus, the question that could be posed to Muslims would be, 'What is salvation?' The Christian response might be that only God can save us. A prophet or teacher of righteousness cannot be the redeemer of the world. If, then, Christ is to be our Savior, he must be fully and completely God. Secondly, salvation must reach the point of human need. Only if Christ is fully and completely human as we are, can we humans share in what Christ has done for us.

Daily Prayer

An admirable feature of Islam is the emphasis on daily prayer; that five times per day is set aside for worship and praise of Allah. Centuries before this Muslim practice, Christians earmarked seven points during the day for the daily 'hours.' Up to the present, the daily non-sacramental worship of the Orthodox faith consists of the following:

Vespers – at dusk
Compline – after the evening meal
Midnight service – at midnight or the middle of the night
Matins – at sunrise
1ˢᵗ Hour – around 7AM
3ʳᵈ Hour – around 9AM
6ᵗʰ Hour – around 12 noon
9ᵗʰ Hour – around 3PM

Through these devotional practices, "the remembrance of Christ permeates the whole of life to preserve it from sin and to bless and sanctify all daily activity and labor" (Alkiviadis Calivas). Both the Hebrew and Christian Scriptures encourage us to raise our awareness of the presence of God throughout the day:

"...bless the Lord at all times" —Psalm 34:1
"...seven times a day will I bless you" —Psalm 119:164
"...pray unceasingly" —1st Thessalonians 5:17

Each of the Hours is numbered in accordance with intervals of the day as they were named in antiquity: the First (sunrise), the Third (around 9AM), the Sixth (around 12 noon), and the Ninth (around 3PM). Each Hour has a set of psalms, hymns, and a distinctive prayer for that Hour. Each Hour has a particular theme based upon some aspect of the life of Jesus Christ and His saving work for us. The general themes of each of the Hours are: the coming of the true light (First); the descent of the Holy Spirit on Pentecost (Third); the crucifixion and passion of the Lord (Sixth); and, the death and burial of the Lord (Ninth). For a complete study on the daily services of the Orthodox Church, please refer to *The Liturgikon*, published by Antakya Press.

God vs. Allah

There are numerous attractive characteristics of Islam that all Christians should take note of. Generally speaking, Muslims display a sense of urgency and intensity in the practice of their faith. A Muslim who diligently exercises the Five Pillars models a discipline that all Christians should esteem.

Perhaps if Christians were better versed in the basics of their own faith, we might see fewer lukewarm members. I attended a conference once in which a former Muslim elaborated on his conversion to Christianity. Many times it takes someone from the 'outside' to witness to the faithful.

For example, the speaker noted that there is very little written in the *Quran* about the love of Allah. There is no understanding of a personal relationship with Allah. The speaker went on to highlight that in Islam, the human person is not created in the image of Allah.

Less conciliatory is the emphasis that other religions are dismissed out of hand by Muslims. Many scholars find the negative portion of the *Shahadah* (there is no God but God . . .) very important, since it unequivocally rejects other people's gods. Simply put, the focus of Islam is law and obedience to Allah.

The Gospel, or 'Good News' offered to humankind is that God is love: "God so loved the world that He sent His only begotten Son, that whoever believes in Him will not perish but have everlasting life" (John 3:16). Christianity offers the image of the Loving Father of the Prodigal Son, a father (God) who respects our freedom and waits for a loving response. The Gospel of Jesus Christ extends the virtues of compassion, forgiveness, hope, and transformation. We can have a personal relationship with God because Jesus has broken the barriers of sin and death through the power of His resurrection.

The facet of Christianity that should distinguish itself from any religion in the world, including Islam, is joy. Rev. Alexander Schmemann, in his book *The Life of the World*, summarizes this point beautifully:

> . . .from the very beginning Christianity has been the proclamation of joy, of the only possible joy on earth...Let us, therefore, forget for a while the technical discussions about the Church, its mission, its methods. Not that these discussions are wrong or unnecessary – but they can be useful and meaningful only within a fundamental context, and that context is the 'great joy' from which everything else in Christianity developed and acquired its meaning.

"For behold, I bring you good tidings of great joy" – thus begins the Gospel, and its end is: "And they worshipped him and returned to Jerusalem with great joy." And we must recover the meaning of this great joy…Joy, however, is not something one can define or analyze. One enters into joy: "Enter thou into the joy of the Lord."

KEY TERMS

Allah – the Arabic word for 'the God.'

Hadith – texts not found in the Quran containing traditional reports of Muhammad's words and example, taken by Muslims as a foundation for conduct and doctrine.

Hajj – one of the Five Pillars that calls for a Muslim's pilgrimage to Mecca.

Hijrah – Muhammad's departure from Mecca to Medina in 622.

Imam – a spiritual guide in Shiite Islam.

Islam – translated from the Arabic as 'complete trusting surrender to God.'

Jihad – a Muslim term meaning holy struggle, warfare in defense, or pursuit, of a good cause.

Kabah – a cubical temple in Mecca said to have been built by Abraham.

Muslim – a submitter to God; a follower of Islam and the Prophet Muhammad.

Quran – the scriptures of Islam translated as 'reading' or 'reciting'.

Ramadan – the Muslim lunar month during which the faithful are expected to fast from sunup to sundown.

Salat – the prescribed daily prayers for Muslims.

Sawm – the Arabic word for fasting.

Shahadah – Declaring one's faith, 'bearing witness' as a Muslim. The brief declaration formula is a twofold profession of faith: in God as the only God, and in Muhammad as God's prophet.

Shariah – the specific regulations and conduct of Islamic law.

Shiite – a minority branch of Islam which holds that Muhammad's genuine successors descended from his son-in-law Ali.

Sufism – the devotional, ascetic, or mystical movement within Islam.

Sunni – the majority branch of Islam, which holds that genuine succession from Muhammad does not depend on hereditary descent.

Sura – a chapter of the Quran.

Zakat – one of the Five Pillars that involves alms.

SELECT WRITINGS IN ISLAM

The Fatihah (Opening)

In the Name of God, the merciful Lord of mercy. Praise be to God, the Lord of all being, the merciful Lord of mercy, Master of the Day of Judgment. You alone we serve and to You alone we come for aid. Guide us in the straight path, the path of those whom You have blessed, not of those against whom there is displeasure, nor of those who have gone astray.

The Nature of God

Say, "God is One, the Eternal God. He begot none, nor was He begotten. None is equal to Him."

Say, "Praise be to God who has never begotten a son; who has no partner in His Kingdom; who needs none to defend Him from humiliation."

Scriptures in History

We have revealed the Torah, in which there is guidance and light. By it the prophets who surrendered themselves judged the Jews …according to God's Book which had been committed to their keeping and to which they themselves were witnesses…After them We sent forth Jesus, the son of Mary, confirming the Torah already revealed, and gave him the Gospel, in which there is guidance and light, corroborating what was revealed before it in the Torah, a guide and an admonition to the righteousness…And to you (Muslims) We have revealed the Book with the truth. It confirms the Scriptures which came before it and stands as a guardian over them.

Jihad (exertion, struggle, holy war)

Fight for the sake of God those that fight against you, but do not attack them first. God does not love the aggressors.

Permission to take up arms is hereby given to those who are attacked, because they have been wronged.

For those who are slain in the course of God, He will not allow their works to perish. He will vouchsafe them guidance and ennoble their state; He will admit them to the Paradise he has made known to them.

On humility

Do not treat men with scorn, nor walk proudly on the earth: God does not love the arrogant and the vainglorious. Rather let your gait be modest and your voice low: the harshest of voices is the braying of the ass.

Right speech

God does not love harsh words, except when uttered by a man who is truly wronged

A kind word with forgiveness is better than charity followed by an insult

On the role of women

For Muslim men and women, for believing men and women, for devout men and women, for truthful men and women, for men and women who are patient and constant, for men and women who humble themselves, for men and women who give charity, for men and women who fast, for men and women who engage much in Allah's praise – for them has Allah prepared forgiveness and great reward.

Men have authority over women because Allah has made the one superior to the other, and because they spend their wealth to maintain them. Good women are obedient. They guard their unseen parts because Allah has guarded them. As for those from whom you fear disobedience, admonish them and send them to beds apart and beat them. Then if they obey you, take no further action against them.

QUESTIONS FOR REFLECTION

1) How does Abraham's role in Judaism, Jesus' role in Christianity, and Muhammad's role in Islam differ from each other?

2) What are the assets and liabilities in the Muslim idea of a theocracy with no separation between religion and politics? What role should religion play in public and government life?

3) Compare the Five Pillars of Islam with the requirements found in Judaism and Christianity.

4) In your opinion, what ideals of Islam attract universal respect? Which ideals of Islam interfere with people's embracing it?

APPENDIX I

WORLDWIDE RELIGIOUS ADHERENTS – 2006*

Christianity	2.1 billion
Islam	1.3 billion
Hinduism	850 million
Buddhism	375 million
Primal Religions	300 million
Sikhism	23 million
Judaism	15 million
Baha'i	7 million
Jainism	4 million
Shinto	4 million
Neo-paganism	1 million
Scientology	.5 million

Confucianism and Taoism are not listed with specific figures. Determining estimates for these two religions are difficult for a variety of reasons. China is not forthcoming with basic information about their country, including religion. Only in recent years has the government begun to open its borders to economic, cultural, and religious interactions. Further complicating the issue of specific figures for Confucianism and Taoism is that many Asian people practice a blending of various religions, combining Confucianism and Taoism with folk religion, divination, Buddhism, and other spiritual expressions.

---

* Encyclopedia Britannica

Alexander Goussetis

To place Chinese religious life in perspective, consider this historical fact. For the better part of 2500 years, civil servants in China were required to undergo exams based on Confucianism and the cultural classics synthesized by Confucius. When one considers the population of China throughout these past two and one-half millennia, together with its current population, the impact of Confucianism in that culture is immense.

APPENDIX II

RESOURCES FOR FURTHER STUDY

Primal Religions

Gill, Sam. *Native American Religions*. Belmont, CA: Wadsworth, 1982.

Knudson, Peter, and David Suzuki. *Wisdom of the Elders*. Toronto: Stoddart, 1993.

Mbiti, John. *Introduction to African Religion*. London: Heinemann, 1992.

Tedlock, Dennis, and Barbara Tedlock, eds. *Teachings from the American Earth: Indian Religion and Philosophy*. New York: Liveright, 1992.

Hinduism

Basham, Arthur L. *The Wonder That Was India*. New York: Grove, 1959.

Eck, Diana L. *Banaras: City of Light*. New York: Columbia University Press, 1998.

Eliade, Mircea. *Yoga: Immortality and Freedom*. Princeton: Princeton University Press, 1991.

Harvey, Andrew. *Hidden Journey: A Spiritual Awakening*. New York: Arkana/Penguin, 1992.

Buddhism

deBarry, William Theodore, ed. *The Buddhist Tradition in India, China, & Japan*. New York: Random House, 1972.

Jones, Ken. *The Social Face of Buddhism: An Approach to Social and Political Activity*. London: Wisdom, 1989.

Rahula, Walpola. *What the Buddha Taught*. New York: Grove Press, 1987.

Tiyavanich, Kamala. *Forest Recollections*. Honolulu: University of Hawaii Press, 1997.

Jainism

Dundas, Paul. *The Jains*. London: Routledge, 1993.

Jaini, P. S. *The Jaina Path of Purification*. Berkeley: University of California Press, 1979.

Koller, John. *The Indian Way*. New York: Macmillan, 1982.

Confucianism

Fingarette, Herbert. *Confucius: The Secular as Sacred*. New York: Harper and Row, 1972.

Taylor, Rodney. *The Religious Dimensions of Confucianism*. Albany: State University of New York Press, 1990.

Thompson, Laurence G. *Chinese Religion: An Introduction*, fifth edition. Belmont, CA: Wadsworth, 1996.

Tu Wei-ming. *Confucian Thought: Selfhood as Creative Transformation*. Albany: State University of New York Press, 1985.

Taoism

Kohn, Livia. *The Taoist Experience: An Anthology*. Albany: State University of New York Press, 1993.

Liu I-Ming. *Awakening to the Tao*. Translated by Thomas Cleary. Boston: Shambala, 1988.

Porter, Bill. *Road to Heaven: Encounters with Chinese Hermits*. San Francisco: Mercury House, 1993.

Schipper, Kristofer. *The Taoist Body*. Berkeley: University of California Press, 1993.

Judaism

Berger, Alan L. ed., *Judaism in the Modern World*. New York: New York University Press, 1994.

Heschel, Abraham J. *Between God and Man: An Interpretation of Judaism*. New York: The Free Press, 1959.

Jacobs, Louis. *Principles of the Jewish Faith*. Northvale, New Jersey: Jason Aronson, 1988.

Seltzer, Robert. *Jewish People, Jewish Thought: The Jewish Experience in History*. New York: Macmillan, 1980.

Islam

Akbar Ahmed. *Living Islam*. New York: Facts on File, 1994.

Denny, Frederick. *Islam and the Muslim Community*. Prospect, IL: Waveland, 1998.

Esposito, John. Islam: *The Straight Path*, 3rd ed. New York: Oxford University Press, 1998.
Schimmel, Annemarie. *Islam: An Introduction*. Albany: State University of New York Press, 1992.

Orthodox Christianity and other faiths

Clapsis, Emmanuel. *The Orthodox Church in a Pluralistic World*. WCC Publications, 2004

_____ . *Orthodoxy in Converation*. WCC Publications, 2000.

Garvey, John. *Seeds of the Word: Orthodox Thinking on Other Religions*. Crestwood: St. Vladimir's Seminary Press, 2005.

Schmemann, Alexander. *Church, World, Mission*. Crestwood: St. Vladimir's Seminary Press, 1979.

Yannoulatos, Archbishop Anastasios. *Facing the World*. Crestwood: St. Vladimir's Seminary Press, 2003.

Alexander Goussetis